# CREATIVE DIRECTION IN A DIGITAL WORLD

## A GUIDE TO BEING A MODERN CREATIVE DIRECTOR

# CREATIVE DIRECTION IN A DIGITAL WORLD

## A GUIDE TO BEING A MODERN CREATIVE DIRECTOR

**Adam Harrell**

CRC Press
Taylor & Francis Group
Boca Raton London New York

CRC Press is an imprint of the
Taylor & Francis Group, an **informa** business

A CHAPMAN & HALL BOOK

CRC Press
Taylor & Francis Group
6000 Broken Sound Parkway NW, Suite 300
Boca Raton, FL 33487-2742

© 2017 by Taylor & Francis Group, LLC
CRC Press is an imprint of Taylor & Francis Group, an Informa business

No claim to original U.S. Government works

Printed on acid-free paper
Version Date: 20160616

International Standard Book Number-13: 978-1-138-84751-4 (Paperback)

### Library of Congress Cataloging-in-Publication Data

Names: Harrell, Adam, author.
Title: Creative direction in a digital world : a guide to being a modern creative director / author: Adam Harrell.
Description: Boca Raton : Taylor & Francis, CRC Press, 2017.
Identifiers: LCCN 2016024073 | ISBN 9781138847514 (alk. paper)
Subjects: LCSH: Web sites--Design. | Computer animation. | Creativity in advertising. | Internet advertising. | Internet marketing. | Video recordings--Production and direction.
Classification: LCC TK5105.888 .H373 2017 | DDC 659.14/4--dc23
LC record available at https://lccn.loc.gov/2016024073

**Visit the Taylor & Francis Web site at**
**http://www.taylorandfrancis.com**

**and the CRC Press Web site at**
**http://www.crcpress.com**

# Contents

## SECTION I   Learn and Design

## SECTION II    Building and Showing

# Preface

*Creative Direction in a Digital World* provides designers the tools they need to craft compelling digital experiences across screens, devices, and platforms.

Readers will learn how to take a multidisciplinary, human-centered approach to digital creative direction that will help them uncover target audience insights, conceive more creative campaigns, change consumer behavior, and create more user-friendly digital experiences.

This book:

- Shows designers how to understand the client's biggest challenges and distill insights about the audience into creative strategies and digital experiences that get results.
- Teaches designers how to communicate their ideas to a skeptical client and provides advice on managing a creative team.
- Is divided into 10 chapters that focus on different key aspects of the creative director's job from start to finish.
- Works with a companion website that provides assets such as sample creative briefs, buyer journey maps, and interviews with other digital creative directors about how all of these skills are put into action on a day-to-day basis.

**Adam Harrell**
*Founder, Nebo Agency, Atlanta, GA*

# About the Author

**Adam Harrell** is the president and founder of Nebo, Atlanta, GA; he leads brand strategy and creative direction for one of the largest independent digital agencies in the Southeast. A 15-year digital veteran, he speaks frequently on the topics of human-centered design, brand strategy, user experience, and interactive storytelling.

Adam earned a bachelor's degree in Political Science & International Relations from Appalachian State University, Boone, North Carolina. He was named one of Atlanta's "40 under 40" rising stars by the *Atlanta Business Chronicle* in 2011, selected as the Atlanta AMA's Agency Marketer of the Year in 2013, the 2013 Interactive Marketer of the Year by the Atlanta Interactive Marketing Association, and the 2014 Digital Marketer of the Year by the Technology Association of Georgia. He also teaches interactive design at the Creative Circus—one of the nation's premier portfolio schools.

# Introduction

*If we did all the things we are capable of doing, we would literally astonish ourselves.*

*Thomas Edison*

Thanks to *Mad Men*, when we think of the role of a creative director, we think of Don Draper. The brilliant creative taking drinks from a bottle of scotch, writing commercials, and solving advertising riddle after advertising riddle for big brand name companies.

It was a role that thrived in a mass media marketing world where TV was the king, and the mediums of print and radio were close behind. But the days of mass media are over, and so is the role of the traditional creative director. No longer can you tell a single story in a 30 second format and buy your way into the public's consciousness. In the modern world, attention, not media, is our most scarce resource.

We're now firmly entrenched in the middle of a digital revolution that has resulted in more screens, more platforms, and more device types than ever before. Along with this paradigm shift, a new role has emerged—that of the digital creative director.

The role of digital creative director is to act as the auteur of these complex digital experiences: To understand the client's biggest challenges and distill insights about the audience into creative strategies and digital experiences that get results.

A digital creative director must come up with big ideas, solve hard problems, be creative, and make things happen. With this comes a responsibility to avoid complacency and the easy way out—to create things that add value. Not noise.

Success in this role requires more than being able to push pixels, design interfaces, or craft headlines. It requires the ability to craft experiences. Experiences that speak to the heart, change minds, and change behaviors. You must understand your audience, drive brand strategy, come up with big ideas in a short period of time, craft compelling stories, and find ways to make your message spread.

You also have to be able to communicate your ideas to a skeptical audience. Our profession is at heart a rhetorical one. If you can't sell your concepts with clarity and passion, then they will likely die in the murky waters of client indecision. As Luke Sullivan said about pitching an idea to clients, "We're selling invisible poetry machines to scientists" (Curl 2011). It's sad to think that your idea is only as good as the way you pitch it, but it's true.

However, as a digital creative director, your responsibility doesn't end with the presentation of ideas. Ideas are not enough.

To be a good digital creative director, you have to be able to produce your ideas and ensure the execution of those ideas is as remarkable as the idea itself. Much like an executive chef is responsible for the quality of what comes out of his kitchen, the digital creative director has to do the same in regard to the experiences he crafts.

You have to be able to understand and manage the digital design process from start to finish. To overcome obstacles, understand constraints and create great work in spite of the pressure toward mediocrity.

Owing to the complexity of digital experiences, many things can go wrong. And make no mistake—things will go wrong. As a result, there will be many opportunities to avoid responsibility, to play the victim and blame others for why your work isn't great. The client was too small, the account people are lazy, or the developer sucked. But at the end of the day the digital creative director looks in the mirror and says, "I take responsibility for the outcome. It's my job to make it remarkable."

There will be times where you will be tired, burnt out, and at the end of your rope—but with the right attitude and approach you can keep yourself and your team happy through even the most troubled waters, acting as shock absorber in bad times and as a guard against complacency in good times.

This book is divided into 10 chapters, and each chapter focuses on a different aspect of the job. I wrote this book in sequence, but I tried to ensure that each chapter could stand on its own so that readers could easily use them as a reference.

Chapter 1 is about understanding your audience and building empathy, so that you can design experiences that connect with them.

Chapter 2 is a high-level overview of brand strategy and how to guide clients on positioning and differentiating their brand.

Chapter 3 is all about coming up with ideas. It covers practical tips on problem solving and the ideation process.

Chapter 4 is about design—more specifically it's about the key elements and attributes of great design along with a number of examples for inspiration.

Chapter 5 is about how to use design to change behavior and build habits, including practical tips on getting your audience to take a desired action.

Chapter 6 shows why content is what differentiates a great digital experience from a mediocre one, and how to create content that your audience will love.

Chapter 7 is full of practical advice on how to get your message to spread and win the war for attention.

Chapter 8 dives deep into the details of the design process and provides advice on how you can make the work better each and every step along the way.

Chapter 9 will provide you a framework for presenting your ideas like a pro and provide an outline for you to work from for creative presentations.

Chapter 10 is about you and your team. More specifically, how to keep yourself motivated, your team happy, and build a strong creative culture.

I wrote this book as a guide to help others who want to take on the challenge of being a digital creative director. This book contains no shortcuts or secrets. Just a bit of hard won advice that I wanted to share.

Thanks for reading, and I hope you enjoy it.

## Reference

Curl, B. February 24, 2011. Luke Sullivan sells invisible poetry machines to scientists. Curl Talk. http://blog.brandoncurl.com/2011/02/24/luke-sullivan-sells-invisible-poetry-machines-to-scientists/. Accessed on January 29, 2016.

# Acknowledgments

Thank you for reading this book.

I wrote this book to share all the things I wish I had known when I first started my career. I've never written anything longer than 20 pages, so the idea of writing an entire book was intimidating. I hope it helps you in your craft and that you enjoy reading it.

The experience of writing it is one that I'll cherish. I spent almost every weekend over the course of eight long months working on it. A few hundred hours went into its production, and it has been a product of over a decade of experience.

Thanks to my wife Alison. Without her love and support, I would be half the man I am today. She's the best wife, mother, and friend that a husband could ask for.

Thanks to my brother and business partner Brian. It's been a pleasure working alongside him and growing both personally and professionally in the process. Without him, Nebo wouldn't be what it is today.

Thanks to Mason Brown, whose detailed feedback and notes on early drafts helped me clarify my thinking and dramatically improved the final outcome.

Thanks to my good friend Holt Lyda for being my creative copilot on many an awesome endeavor. There's no one I'd rather fight alongside of in the creative trenches.

Thanks to Zach Graham for helping design the cover of this book. He's one amazing dude, even though his dog's feet smell like Fritos.

To my daughter Adeline; she was barely a year old when I started writing this book. Now she's almost three. I can't wait to see the incredible things her future holds.

To the rest of my family: Mom, Dad, Fred, Melissa, Aaron, Daniel, and Marilynn as well as Al, Joan, Christie, and Michael—thank you all for your support and love. When I think of you all, I realize I just might be the luckiest man alive.

Finally, I'd like to thank all the fine folks who have worked at Nebo over the years. It's an honor to have worked beside each and every one of you.

Thank you again for reading. Since feedback is the only way to improve. I'd love to hear your thoughts on the book. Feel free to send me praise, or hate mail. My email address is adam@neboagency.com.

# Section I

# Learn and Design

# Chapter 1

# Understand Your Audience

*There is nothing so terrible as activity without insight.*

**Johann Wolfgang von Goethe**

Empathy is at the heart of creativity. If you can understand what others see, think, and feel—their needs, wants, fears, and aspirations—then you can design an experience that will connect with them.

Luckily human beings are born to be empathetic. Our brains actually have a special set of neurons called *mirror neurons* designed specifically for the task. They recognize the feelings of others and help us understand their intentions.

So if empathy is important and humans are good at it, then why is empathy often missing from creative work? The simplest explanation is that too often we're designing experiences for ourselves. We get so caught up in the act of creating something that we forget who will actually be using it. We assume that everyone uses technology like we do and that we share a common worldview.

This is a dangerous habit. The best creative work is rooted in a deep understanding of the audience, but you can only gain this understanding if you seek it out.

In this chapter, we'll talk about the role that insights play in the creative process, the basic process of user research, and how findings can be shared via audience personas and buyer journey maps.

## Insights Only Appear When You're Looking for Them

Insights can be found anywhere, but they're always hidden. If they weren't hard to find, they wouldn't be valuable. Your job is to root them out of their holes and drag them kicking and screaming into the light of day.

To find an insight, start by thinking about the customer and what they care about. Put yourself in their shoes. Imagine their lives—their hopes, their fears, and their worldview. Find the places they congregate and observe them carefully.

How would they describe themselves? What tribes do they belong to? How do they perceive the product or service? What are the pain points they have that the product or service solves? How would they describe it to a friend? What basic human desire are they trying to solve through their purchase? How considered is the purchase?

Start asking these questions, and listen carefully. Then start thinking about it and don't stop until you've found something meaningful.

By building empathy and finding insights you can make anything better, faster, smarter, easier, more usable, and more meaningful. It just takes effort to do so.

There's no secret process to finding insights. Tenacity is the best advice I can give.

For instance, if you're building a campaign for a major sunglasses brand then you might start by asking a customer why they chose a specific brand. The answer would probably be rather rational—something like *they were on sale*.

This type of observation isn't very valuable. But, if you were to dig deeper and follow up each answer by asking them why, then something interesting happens. You start to get a deeper insight into how they view themselves and your product.

For example, Why did you buy them when you saw them on sale? Well, I've always liked the look. They're a classic style. I like things that are timeless. Why is that important? Since it means they're not going out of style. If I'm spending $300 on a pair of sunglasses I want to be able to wear them for a long time.

*Why* is a powerful question that allows you to go beyond the initial answer and get to the root of the problem.

Sakichi Toyoda—the founder of Toyota and the father of the Japanese Industrial Revolution—was the first to document the power of asking why (Ohno 2006).

He cut his teeth building weaving devices and looms. When trying to perfect an automated loom, he actually conducted a yearlong experiment that had his looms running against his competitors in a real-world environment. As each of his looms failed he focused on how to improve their performance.

The methodology he used was simple. Like any good problem solver, he started by asking *Why*. But, he realized that you can't get to the root of the problem with a single question. A single question only identifies the symptom, not the root problem.

Like a child trying to figure out why the sky is blue, he repeated the question *why?* a minimum of five times in order to get to the root of the problem. This simple insight was the birth of what is known today as *the 5 Whys method*.

Why did the loom break? Because the gear jammed. Why did the gear jam? Because it ran out of oil. Why did it run out of oil? Because the operator didn't add it. Why does the operator need to add oil? Because oil isn't automatically added. Why isn't oil automatically added? Because there isn't an oil pump.

Sakichi's method of root cause analysis is now taught in MBA programs around the world. But, his genius wasn't related to some magic insight. The *5 Whys* method is applied common sense.

Its development was the result of his fierce tenacity in trying to get to the root of his problems. This same approach to problem solving applies to finding insights.

## Don't Be a Segway

In 2001, one of the most hyped products of my lifetime was launched. *TIME* magazine ran a cover story entitled "Reinventing the Wheel" about a revolutionary new form of transport (Heilemann 2001). In fact, many said the company that made this revolutionary product would be the fastest company ever to reach $1 billion in sales. This product was the Segway.

The Segway, which is now seen as the transportation of choice for mall cops and city tours, is actually a pretty amazing piece of engineering. It's self-balancing, rechargeable, and easy to learn to use. In fact the inventor was so confident in his product he stated that the Segway "will be to the car what the car was to the horse and buggy." It would usher in a whole new transportation revolution as cars would get banned from city roads and replaced with Segways.

So why didn't the Segway live up to the hype? How did it become the Ford Edsel of the dot com generation? The Segway is a great example of the danger of designing products based on a flawed understanding of the people who would actually use it. They were so concerned with being the first to bring their invention to market that they actually designed it in secret. They didn't seek feedback.

The result was a product that wasn't built for the real world. The Segway didn't protect the user in the rain. It was too big for crowded sidewalks and too small for roads. It was too heavy to store easily. People riding them looked a bit goofy.

If they'd been less concerned with secrecy and done proper audience research, they would have realized some of these flaws and could have iterated toward a solution. Instead they focused on raising money, building hype, and trying to invent the next great transportation revolution in isolation.

## Research without Insight Is Wasted

Years ago I was working with a major hotel group on a rebranding effort for one of their most successful brands. As part of this effort, they undertook a global research effort to guide their messaging and positioning.

They conducted a quantitative and qualitative research effort that spanned the globe. Focus groups, surveys, and every other form of market research technique was used during the project.

After hearing about this giant research effort, I was excited to see the results. After all, millions of dollars spent on research would definitely lead to some exciting insights.

So we gathered the teams in a conference room and the research findings were presented. Out of 100 plus slides, probably 30 had to do with how the research was conducted: descriptions of the techniques and maps of where it was conducted. The next 30 slides were pull quotes from interviews and survey result summaries.

Then we got to the analysis section. Years of research finally leading to what we were told would be a brilliant conclusion that would help differentiate and revitalize the brand.

So what was the result of all this research? The key finding was that life in a hotel is different from life at home, and that people prefer to stay at places where they can relax and feel comfortable.

I remember looking at my buddy Holt and just shaking my head. All that effort expended and that was the insight! Now don't get me wrong, the statement is accurate, but it's also not an insight worthy of the millions of dollars they spent on research.

An insight should shape your creative strategy in a meaningful way. It should make one stop and think: *I've never thought it that way.* It should challenge an existing belief and make you rethink your approach.

If an insight doesn't change what you're doing, it's not an insight.

## Don't Confuse Customer Research with Science

The reason most people don't do customer research is it's intimidating. They think it has to be scientific. That's what leads to millions of dollars being extended to triple check your findings in every country around the globe.

The goal of customer research in human-centered design isn't to increase the world's knowledge on a particular topic. It's not academic. It's not research for research sake. The goal is to do just enough to help you make a great customer experience. No more, no less.

As a creative director, you may or may not have a say in the types of research that are conducted, but you do need to understand the tools and techniques that are available to your team.

The first type of research is quantitative. Quantitative research is all about hard data. This means big sample sizes and standardized survey questions. Political polling is an example of quantitative research. It's great for seeing how you stack up against the competition: measuring brand awareness, customer satisfaction, and other easily quantifiable metrics. It's not so great at helping you understand what the customer thinks or feels through the buyer journey, identifying pain points, creative tension, or understand why they buy or don't buy.

That's where qualitative research comes in. Qualitative research is generally a much smaller sample size—sometimes as few as 5 to 10 people total. Instead of tightly defined survey questions, the discussion is generally more loosely structured so that the interviewer is free to explore different topics.

Unfortunately, qualitative research has bad reputation in the creative community for one simple reason: focus groups.

Focus groups have become so widespread because decision makers use them to cover their a** in case something doesn't work. They're the primary tool of a risk-averse corporate culture. *I don't know where we went wrong. The focus groups loved it* is a built-in excuse for an executive who doesn't want to take responsibility for their own creative work.

That's why Steve Jobs abhorred the focus group and Henry Ford was rumored to have said, "If I had asked people what they wanted, they would have said faster horses" (Vlaskovits 2011).

## Why Focus Groups Fail and an Easier Alternative

Focus groups fail to generate valuable insights for a few key reasons.

First, consumers often have other less than sincere motivations for answering and participating in focus groups. The screening process is far from perfect. In fact many research companies send screeners out to a single list of semiprofessional respondents.

Will Leitch writing about his experience as a semiprofessional focus group member in the *New York Magazine* put it this way:

In one (focus) group for Johnnie Walker Black, it was obvious the marketers wanted us to consider their beverage upscale, for special occasions. Recognizing this, I made up a story about learning my best friend was engaged and telling him, "It's Johnnie Walker time!" The interviewer looked like he wanted to hug me.

It's also important to be vague. During the focus group on travel, the interviewer asked me if there were any countries I might have moral qualms visiting. The correct answer was, "Oh, none at all." But I blurted out, "South Africa," sharing some underdeveloped thoughts I had about apartheid. The interviewer's face sharpened, and he began to pepper me with questions.

I had forgotten the cardinal rule: They don't want your opinion; they want you to confirm what they already think. You're whatever they want you to be, baby. (Leitch 2014)

The second reason focus groups fail to generate insight is people can't predict what they want and don't understand their own motives. Humans have an amazing capability for rationalization. It's an innate defense mechanism. If you ask someone why he or she did something it's rare that they will answer accurately and objectively. Instead they'll answer in the way that puts their actions in the most positive possible light. Most people simply want to please. They want to make you happy with answers you'll find acceptable. After all—people are irrational. The idea that they can provide rational explanations for irrational behaviors and biases that they may not even be aware of is a real challenge.

When you add in the effects of social dynamics, these behaviors become even more pronounced. Whether it's because of a participant's desire to maintain a certain image, give the politically correct answer, or just fit in with the rest of the group, people are unlikely to share their true feelings in a roomful of strangers.

Lastly, focus groups fail because they assume that all consumer input is valid. It's an accepted rule of market research that if you ask someone a question, they'll always attempt to answer it. Even if they have absolutely no idea what you're talking about.

Now some will argue that the focus group has its place. That it can be used to take the pulse of culture, or test concepts. However, these questions can be tackled other ways as well without all the downsides of focus groups.

Instead of focus groups I prefer real-world field observation and one-on-one qualitative interviews.

Field observation means that instead of asking people what they do, you can actually watch them. Great creativity—like great comedy—often arises from a universal truth. So observation is perhaps one of the most important skills in the creative directors' toolbox. It's also the simplest form of research. So even if you don't have budget, you can still do field research.

Find out where your target audience hangs out (online and offline) and observe them. See how they talk, what they care about, how they view the world, and what they value. This way you can make sure that the messages you craft will resonate.

If you want to conduct primary customer research, then one-on-one interviews are a great way to go. They allow you to remove the problem of social dynamics, and because you only need a small sample size of 5 to 15 people, they're easy to recruit, conduct, and manage.

To help find and recruit research participants you can use web-based tools like ethn.io—which is a piece of javascript that goes on a website and randomly directs users to a short survey that will help you learn a little more about the respondent to see if they may be a good fit for your research. The benefit of this approach is that you're talking to people who are actually using your site.

You can also recruit by posting your screener to craigslist, trade forums, or other places that your audience gathers.

When conducting the interview, be sure to create a discussion guide to explore the topics that are important, but be prepared to wander off topic and explore tangents relevant to your work.

When done properly, you should spend more time listening than talking. And don't forget to record the interview. It's really hard to take notes and be a good listener at the same time.

## The Right and Wrong Way to Do Audience Personas

Once you've developed an understanding of your audience, you'll want to document those findings in an easy-to-share and understandable form. As a creative director you need to be able to craft a good persona. It's an important skill that will serve you well.

Alan Cooper is credited as the father of user personas, and he helped introduce them to the software world in 1999 after he published his book, *The Inmates Are Running the Asylum* (Alan 2004). After his book was published, personas became all the rage at software companies.

However, not all personas are created equal. Too often personas are focused on the narrative about an idealized user. They tell you all about the audience with flowing prose that speaks of the *empowered mom* who carefully chooses only the best organic ingredients for her family. Personas like this are works of fiction. Not design tools.

A good persona should help your team make important decisions such as what content to create or features to prioritize. It should help guide a team to the right design decision. It should introduce the audience's worldview and speak clearly to their life goals, experience goals, end goals, pain points, and concerns.

Life goals are what they're looking to do with their life. These are the things that the target audience actually cares about at this specific point in their life. Being a good father, providing for your family, or leaving a lasting legacy are examples of life goals that someone may have.

Experience goals are how they want to feel during the actual experience. If it's a game, then they want to be immersed in another world and escape their day-to-day existence. If it's a digital experience in the financial industry, they may want to feel optimistic about their financial future, in control and secure.

End goals are the things they are actually trying to accomplish. These are the objectives they have and tasks they're trying to complete during the digital experience. If you're designing a digital experience for a library system, it could be finding research materials. If you're creating a new website in the travel industry, it could be planning the perfect trip.

A good persona should also speak to the individual's concerns and pain points. What are they afraid of, what keeps them up at night, and what problems can you help solve?

Here are two example personas for different user types of a university library website (Figures 1.1 and 1.2).

**Dr. Andrea Price**

Andrea grew up in a family that broke the conventional "don't talk about politics and religion" rule. She grew up with parents that loved to debate and encouraged intense discussion 24 h a day, 7 days a week.

Today, Andrea puts her upbringing to use as a political science professor at Spelman. She does some research and gets published occasionally, but her main focus is on creating innovative lesson plans and making sense for her students of the world's complex political workings.

Andrea has some great ideas for how she can incorporate more multimedia technology and flip the classroom (deliver online video lectures and spend more time working hands-on in the classroom), but she's not comfortable with recording process or online setup.

**End Goals**
• Reserve a room and record a lecture
• Request new materials for her students

**Experience Goal**
• Avoid feeling confused

**Life Goals**
• Write a novel about Madam C.J. Walker
• Be the best grandmother possible

**FIGURE 1.1    Example persona for college professor.**

**Alexia Anderson**

Alexia is planning to pursue a career in finance; she's currently in her last semester as an accounting major.

As an aspiring accountant, Alexia hasn't spent too much time in the library. She'd rather be leveraging a lengthy formula and crunching numbers than writing a paper. But, in her last semester, Alexia has been assigned a group project that includes a 40-page paper assessing the use of tax avoidance techniques employed by large corporations in the United States, a presentation, and an analysis of an example company's taxes.

Alexia is excited to work with her classmates who are in her group, but she's a little daunted at the prospect of finding the best reference material to draw from. She's also concerned they won't be able to snag collaboration rooms, since other classes are issuing projects around the same time.

**End Goals**

• See when the library closes on Saturday
• Access the latest accounting journals
• Reserve a room for her group

**Experience Goal**

• Feel like she's in control

**Life Goals**

• Graduate Summa Cum Laude
• Get a job at one of the top five accounting firms

FIGURE 1.2    **Example persona for college student.**

## Mapping the Consumer Journey

The buyer journey in the real-world is complex. It spans offline and online as well as across devices and platforms—if we want to truly understand our audience, we also have to understand the journey they take.

In traditional marketing, the buyer journey is defined in a few simple phases: *awareness*, *consideration*, and *decision*. Your goal as a creative director is to design an experience that moves a potential customer from one phase to the next until they finally make a purchase decision (see Figure 1.3).

As you think through these phases, consider how the experience can meet their needs at each stage.

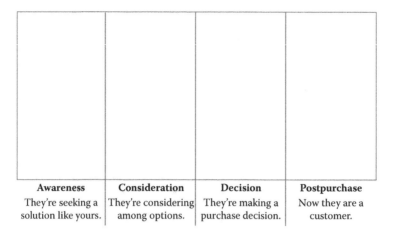

| Awareness | Consideration | Decision | Postpurchase |
|---|---|---|---|
| They're seeking a solution like yours. | They're considering among options. | They're making a purchase decision. | Now they are a customer. |

FIGURE 1.3    **The four phases of the buyer journey.**

Most of the time a consumer isn't seeking out what you're selling. They may have a pain point they'd consider solving, but often they have no idea a solution even exists.

Your challenge is to get their attention and build a relationship by providing something of value. Tell them a great story, help them solve a problem, or connect them with other like-minded people. When attention is a scarce resource, just getting someone to say, *this brand believes the same things I do* is a win.

## The Awareness Phase

Once they're actively seeking a solution like yours, then they're in the awareness phase of the consumer journey. They start by researching options and looking for recommendations from friends who are experts. They're seeking to find out all available options before narrowing down to a list of potential solutions based on the criteria that best fits their needs.

At this phase you want to be clear in what you're offering, how it compares to other options and if it's meant for people like them. The goal is to build credibility. It's not about making a sales pitch, but positioning yourself as an option that should be considered.

For example, if the consumer is looking for a luxury car, then he's probably Googling things like *best luxury cars*, checking out expert sources like *Car and Driver, Edmunds, or Consumer Reports* and asking his or her car enthusiast friends for advice. At this point, they're trying to answer the questions: *What type of car should someone like me drive?*

## The Consideration Phase

The consideration phase is where things start to get serious. The consumer has narrowed the list and is comparing among a small number of products.

Continuing with the car shopping example, this means selecting a short list of cars that fit the shoppers' self-image. At this point, it's time to start searching for local dealerships and scheduling test drives, as well as researching things like reliability, performance stats, and other more granular, detailed comparison items. Often they'll return to Google and search for expert comparisons that will help them decide one way or another.

In the consideration phase, it's all about giving the consumer reasons to justify their decision. Don't assume that the reasons have to be rational. Often the most powerful justifications are emotional. Third-party justifications are also important at this point. You have to remember that we're in a world of almost perfect information on goods and services, so people are unlikely to trust content that feels like marketing.

## The Decision Phase

Finally a decision will be made. A new mom might decide that a Volvo is the perfect car because it has four doors, drives sporty, and is safe. A tech entrepreneur may decide on a Tesla because that's the car that fits his vision of himself—disruptive, fast, and expensive.

But the consumer journey doesn't end at purchase. Your goal is to make the experience remarkable, so you have to think through ways to add delight. Maybe it's as simple as a gift card taped to the gas cap for them to discover a few weeks later, an iPad with the owner's manual preinstalled or inviting them to a special Tesla owner-only cocktail party on a swanky downtown rooftop. It's during the first 60 days of the postpurchase phase that you have the opportunity to turn your consumer into an evangelist for the brand.

## Marketing Isn't About Selling to Customers. It's About Loving and Delighting Them

With all this talk about the buyer journey, I don't want you to get the idea that marketing should be about sales funnels. That's a short-term view that leads to some dangerous thinking (e.g., spamming the crap out of people until they buy).

Marketing when done right is about creating experiences that people love. This can mean surprising and delighting people with the unexpected/ remarkable, or it can mean keeping your promises consistently over a long period of time and loving your customers.

When marketing's *only purpose* becomes driving leads, there is very little room for creativity and the brand will pay a long-term price for their short-term approach.

# References

Alan, C. 2004. *The Inmates Are Running the Asylum: Why High Tech Products Drive Us Crazy and How to Restore the Sanity*, 2nd edn., Pearson Higher Education, Boston, MA.

Heilemann, J. 2001. Reinventing the wheel. *TIME* magazine. http://content.time.com/time/business/article/0,8599,186660-1,00.html. Accessed on April 18, 2016.

Leitch, W. January 18, 2014. Group thinker. *New York Magazine.* http://nymag.com/nymetro/shopping/features/9299/. Accessed on January 29, 2016.

Ohno, T. March 01, 2006. Ask "why" five times about every matter. Toyota Global Website. http://www.toyota-global.com/company/toyota_traditions/quality/mar_apr_2006.html. Accessed on January 2, 2016.

Vlaskovits, P. August 29, 2011. Henry Ford, innovation, and that "Faster Horse" quote. *Harvard Business Review* Blog. http://blogs.hbr.org/2011/08/henry-ford-never-said-the-fast/. Accessed on January 28, 2016.

# Chapter 2

# Brand Strategy

*Advertising is the tax you pay for being unremarkable.*

**Robert Stephens**
(*quoted in Sacks Danielle,*
Fast Company, *2007*)

## What Is a Brand?

If you want to be an effective creative director, you have to understand branding. Clients are going to expect you to be able to guide them on making decisions on positioning, defining, and communicating their brand and what it stands for.

Unfortunately, the word brand is often misused in the design industry. Designers use brand as a synonym for a logo or a corporate identity system, but design elements are not what makes a brand.

A brand is the combined thoughts, feelings, and memories that a consumer has about a company. It's the stories they tell themselves when purchasing your product, or casting a vote for your cause.

Marty Neumeier in his brilliant book, *The Brand Gap* describes a brand as "the gut feeling someone has about a product, service or company" (Neumeier 2003). As he puts it, "a brand is not what *you* say it is, it's what *they* say it is."

So why do we care about branding? Well, brand value is a real thing. If you can help the consumer understand clearly what makes your brand different and better, then you have a competitive advantage. You'll be remembered, instead of being ignored. In a world with millions of products for sale, a strong brand position can help companies stand out in a crowded marketplace.

So if a strong brand is important and we're in a world where a brand's actions matter more than its words, then it follows that finding ways to clearly demonstrate what makes the brand unique is crucial.

## Identifying Opportunities for Differentiation

The first step to making a brand compelling is to figure out what makes it unique. This starts by figuring out who the competitors are. Generally this is pretty obvious, but sometimes your competition isn't other products in the category. It's the status quo.

Once you've developed a list of who your primary competitors are, write down how they position themselves.

### Questions to Ask When Thinking About Competitors

- What message are they communicating on their website and in their ads?
- What feelings are they trying to evoke?
- What are they trying to remind you of?
- How do they describe themselves? How do other people describe them? Is there a difference between the two?
- What do people love about them? What do they hate about them?
- What do they stand for? Do they have a clear worldview? If so, what is it?
- What are the rational reasons people choose to buy their products?
- What are the emotional reasons people choose to buy their products?
- What sort of voice and tone do they use? Are they funny or serious? Do they speak in jargon or do they sound human?
- Does every competitor say the same thing?
- What could you do to be different?

Once you've asked these questions, you should be able to define the brand position of each competitor in the market. Repeat this process for each competitor.

Generally this looks something like the below.

## Sample Brand Positioning for Import Luxury Cars

| Brand | Positioning |
| --- | --- |
| Lexus | Luxury and reliability perfected. |
| Volvo | Safe and practical luxury. |
| BMW | The ultimate driving machine. |
| Mercedes | German engineered luxury. |

By mapping each company's position, you can understand what positions are already occupied. Now you need to start looking for opportunities of differentiation.

## Don't Emulate the Market Leader

The first mistake most people make when undertaking a branding project is trying to emulate the market leader. What works for a market leader won't work for you. You'll end up competing on their terms and they are better at being who they are than you are. Find the things that people dislike most about the market leader and see if there are opportunities to bring those to the forefront. Every successful brand has its detractors.

Find out what drives those detractors and see if there is an opportunity to capitalize on it. If your brand is local and competing against national competitors, then embrace the fact you're local.

One of my favorite local coffee shops in Atlanta is called Octane Coffee. One of their first print ads featured the headline, "Conveniently located between 27 Atlanta-area Starbucks."

This brand position successfully defined Octane as the underdog, local alternative to the big corporate chain. They parlayed what people disliked about the market leader: their size, their success with nontraditional coffee drinkers, and the fact they're on nearly every corner in any big city—into a differentiated position.

Octane became the spot where in-the-know locals went to get their coffee fix.

## Authenticity Is Important

Authenticity is key. If you try to make an old stodgy brand cool through marketing, it will fail. If you try to make a small company appear large, it will fail.

The only sustainable brand position is one based in truth. Customers today are too smart to get fooled by a slick marketing message. The second a customer's experience doesn't align with the way a brand presents itself the brand loses credibility. Honesty is as important for brands as it is for people. Unfulfilled promises pave the path to brand irrelevance.

Part of the reason that authenticity is more important now than it has been in the past is that the Internet has given rise to greater transparency. We're now closer to a world of perfect information about products and services. As Emanuel Rosen and Itamar Simonson point out in their book, *Absolute Value*, the nature of a marketer's relationship to consumers has changed (Simonson and Emanuel 2014).

Consumers now have instant access to reviews of like-minded consumers and experts. When presented with a choice between biased information from a marketer or independent information from consumers and experts, your audience is going to give more credibility to the third-party sources every time.

Recently, I stopped at a neighborhood restaurant that I'd never been to before. As I was pulling up, I noticed their tagline prominently displayed out front. It said "Small Carbon Footprint | Big Local Flavors."

In the same parking lot a Sysco food truck was making a delivery. Sysco is a $44 billion dollar company. Pretty much the exact opposite of the *Farm-to-Table* trend that this cafe was trying to capitalize on.

At this point, the restaurant lost my respect and my future business. When it comes to branding what you do always trumps what you say.

If you try to present yourself in a way that's not authentic, then the truth will come out. No amount of marketing will make it seem like you care about customers if the majority of your actions are designed to rip them off. The walk matters more than the talk.

## Find and Cultivate a Tribe of People with Similar Worldviews

We are now firmly in the age of conspicuous consumption. What we buy says something about who we are. As we discussed in Chapter 1 on the buyer journey, oftentimes the question people ask is a variation of: *What does a person like me buy?*

People want to be a part of a group of people with a similar worldview. Being part of a group helps them define their own identity (Hogg and Levine 2010). That's why they join community groups, root for sports teams, and support political parties. If a brand can identify a tribe of people with a similar worldview and create an experience that resonates with that tribe, then you can be really successful.

Some may say that not all brands can build a tribe, but every brand can reach out and build something of value for a tribe that already exists.

People may not be passionate about motor oil, but they are passionate about cars. They may not be passionate about pots and pans, but they are passionate about cooking. The tribe isn't always about the product itself.

## Take a Stand and Have a Point of View

In order to attract a tribe, it is vital that you have a strong point of view. Great brands have a clear idea of what they stand for. There's a purpose to what they are doing and they represent something bigger than product alone.

Too many companies are scared of actually having a personality. They confuse being interesting with being controversial. They are afraid that having an opinion will alienate an audience. Like a politician who says one thing in front of the labor unions and another thing in front of a roomful of CEOs, many brands try to avoid alienating any potential audience.

The strongest brands do the opposite. They actively look for ways to take a stand against the status quo. They rally behind a cause, have a purpose, and attract a passionate following because of it.

There's a reason that these are the brands people are most passionate about. They offer something more than just a product/service. They offer a coherent worldview that people can rally behind.

Patagonia is an example of a brand that has a clear worldview. Below is its mission statement.

> Build the best product, cause no unnecessary harm, use business to inspire and implement solutions to the environmental crisis. (Patagonia 2010)

As you can see, its mission has an implicit environmentalism. But how do you balance a concern for the environment with a need to sell more consumer products? The rise of a consumerist society has a dramatic negative impact on the environment.

So Patagonia decided to do something about it. It started the Common Threads Initiative focused on reducing needless consumption, teaching people to repair its clothing instead of replacing it, encouraging people to give away their old clothes so they stayed in use, and recycling every product it makes instead of throwing it away.

To announce this initiative, it ran an ad on Black Friday in the *New York Times* asking people not to buy its products. The headline said, "Don't Buy This Jacket" and urged people to avoid needless consumerism on the most consumerist holiday of the year.

It goes on to explain just how much environmental impact is created by manufacturing one of its jackets: "To make it required 135 liters of water, enough to meet the daily needs (three glasses a day) of 45 people. Its journey from its origin as 60% recycled polyester to our Reno warehouse generated nearly 20 pounds of carbon dioxide, 24 times the weight of the finished product. This jacket left behind, on its way to Reno, two-thirds its weight in waste" (Rosenbaum 2012).

Unlike many brands that try to green wash away their unseemly environmental activities, Patagonia is directly confronting them.

It is clearly not afraid to take a stand and the result was 33% increase in sales (Stock 2013). Another recent effort has been its *Vote the Environment* campaign. Digital photo booths in their stores urge customers to take a photo and share that photo on social media along with why and how they're voting for environment-focused causes/candidates.

On account of this approach, it has engaged a really passionate following of brand evangelists. These people want to lead a more active, healthier, and more sustainable life—and Patagonia shares those values.

## Look toward the Past

Oftentimes you can uncover a brand's purpose by looking toward its origin. Founders of successful companies usually have a clear vision and purpose.

Over time that purpose often gets clouded. Managers take the roles once filled by visionaries and the brand no longer stands for anything. They begin to acquire new companies in new markets and the culture gets diluted.

The tattered remains of that original purpose can provide a clue toward discovering what makes the brand unique and relevant in the modern world. You can look for these clues by acting as a historian toward the brand. Look back at the things they originally produced.

Read the founder's writings, or artifacts from the brand's origins and talk to the people that have worked with the company the longest, whether customers or employees. Then leverage that heritage to inform your creative strategy.

Dell is a brand that lost its way in marketing, but their recent efforts to recapture the original entrepreneurial spirit of the company are compelling. The story of a 19-year-old Michael Dell building computers in his dorm room and growing it to a billion dollar company is well-known, so it offers fertile ground for strong creativity.

One of their 2014 campaigns, "Dell Beginnings," celebrates the dinner tables, pizza joints, and garages where the great technology companies that are now its clients were founded. By getting back to its roots, it hit a cultural nerve and in the process racked up over a million views.

## Purposely Break Industry Conventions

Every industry has category conventions that become stale or meaningless. Words, visuals, and ideas lose meaning as they are overused. For example, car commercials often use the same images of vehicles riding through rugged terrain or a city at night. In the B2B world, you'll often hear a lot of

IT companies say *we focus on solving your business problems* or *we create innovative solutions to enable your business.*

Since people are often bombarded with stale category conventions, avoiding them is often the best way to get noticed.

Tesla became one of the worlds most valuable car manufacturers without ever building a single dealership. They looked at the industry and the role of dealership networks in the customer experience, and broke that convention. Instead of building dealerships they sold directly to the consumer via the web.

The Minerva Project, one of the most exciting startups in higher education, looked at the convention of the standard liberal arts education and challenged almost all of them by banning the traditional lecture in favor of intense seminars. It takes no federal funding and has no libraries, gyms or dining halls, and it replaced the traditional ivy-covered college campus with smaller footprint buildings spread across major global cities such as Berlin, Buenos Aires, and Mumbai so that each year students are exposed to a unique international experience.

In the process, the Minerva Project has raised $25 million in funding and received the type of international press coverage that a traditional university would die to get. Had they taken a more conventional route, this never would have happened.

If an archetype exists, try to defy it. The unexpected is always more memorable.

## B2B Doesn't Have to Be Boring

Oftentimes the brands that need the most help don't sell to consumers, they sell to other businesses. You'll hear these business-to-business companies referred to by the acronym B2B.

You can usually spot them by their reliance on cliché business benefits. I can recite these by memory: increased ROI, lowered cost, improved scalability, greater flexibility. Whether they're selling software, hosting, contract manufacturing, or consulting—the benefits always end up being the same, regardless of what the product actually does.

They forget that their target audience is made up of ordinary people who desire nothing more than to learn a little bit more about what their company does in as clear and conversational a manner as possible. Boring business jargon leads to nothing more than a disinterested market and a confused customer.

Volvo Trucks is a great example of how you can take something that's relatively boring and make it interesting. When it launched a new truck model, it included a dynamic steering system that combined conventional hydraulic-powered steering with an electric motor that receives 2000 signals per second from the truck's onboard sensors. This technology allowed for more precise steering.

To their target audience of truck fleet buyers and independent owner–operators, better steering precision is pretty boring. But the way they introduced this technology to the world was anything but. They hired Jean-Claude Van Damme and had him perform a split between two trucks driving in reverse while slowly drifting apart. It was watched more than 75 million times (YouTube 2013a).

And it wasn't just a one-time hit. Most of their videos have over a million views. One video shows their trucks being chased by a herd of bulls through the curvy streets of Spain and yet another has their company president suspended over the ocean from a crane while standing on one of their trucks suspended only by the tow hook (YouTube 2013b). Each of these videos shows a product benefit in a really compelling manner.

B2B doesn't have to be boring. In fact, good B2B is anything but boring.

## Strong Brand = Strong Impact

Crafting a strong, differentiated brand isn't easy, but it's always worth it. The result is work that's as strategic and effective as it is creative. Without a strong brand as a foundation, the impact of any creative effort will fall short of its potential.

## References

Hogg, M. A. and Levine, J. M. 2010. *Encyclopedia of Group Processes & Intergroup Relations*. SAGE Publications, New Delhi, India.

Neumeier, M. 2003. *The Brand Gap: How to Bridge the Distance between Business Strategy and Design; a Whiteboard Overview*. New Riders, Indianapolis, IN.

Patagonia. September 5, 2010. About Patagonia. http://www.patagonia.com/us/patagonia. go?assetid=2047. Accessed on January 20, 2016.

Rosenbaum, J. December 6, 2012. How Patagonia makes more money by trying to make less. http://www.fastcoexist.com/1681023/how-patagonia-makes-more-money-by-trying-to-make-less. Accessed on January 28, 2016.

Sacks, D. November 28, 2007. From hip-hop to Geek wisdom. *Fast Company*. http://www.fastcompany.com/679753/hip-hop-geek-wisdom. Accessed on April 18, 2016.

Simonson, I. and Emanuel, R. 2014. *Absolute Value: What Really Influences Customers in the Age of (nearly) Perfect Information*. Harper Business, New York.

Stock, K. August 28, 2013. *BusinessWeek*. http://www.businessweek.com/articles/2013-08-28/patagonias-buy-less-plea-spurs-more-buying. Accessed on January 28, 2016.

YouTube. November 13, 2013a. Volvo Trucks – The Epic Split Feat. Van Damme (Live Test). https://www.youtube.com/watch?v=M7FIvfx5J10. Accessed on April 18, 2016.

YouTube. November 1, 2013b. Volvo Trucks – The Hook. https://www.youtube.com/watch?v=Jf_wKkV5dwQ. Accessed on May 24, 2016.

YouTube. November 1, 2013. Volvo Trucks – The Hamster Stunt. https://www.youtube.com/watch?v=7N87uxyDQT0. Accessed on May 24, 2016.

# Chapter 3

# The Process of Ideation and Concepting

*The opposite of love isn't hate; it's indifference.*

*Elie Wiesel*
(US News & World Report, *1986*)

Now that we have a deep understanding of our users and a solid brand strategy, it's time to start concepting. This is where the rubber meets the road. It's where you get to exercise your creative muscles and prove that you're a top-notch digital creative director.

Coming up with great concepts isn't as simple as holding a few brainstorming sessions and doing group creative exercises. Often the creative process is the loneliest. It's just you and the eight pounds of flesh in your skull trying to figure out the best way to solve the client's problem.

Steve Hayden, the copywriter who wrote Apple's legendary 1984 Super Bowl Commercial once said, "If you want to be a well paid copywriter, please your client. If you want to be an award-winning copywriter, please yourself. If you want to be a great copywriter, please your readers" (Sullivan 1998).

This same advice applies to us today. If you want to be well-paid, come up with ideas that please your client. If you want to win awards, come up with ideas that please yourself. If you want to be great, come up with ideas that delight your audience.

In this chapter, we'll talk about how to come up with those ideas. We'll cover the ideation process, how to define the problem, the importance of research and inspiration, why creativity is simply a numbers game, how to iterate ideas quickly, and how to give feedback on other people's ideas.

## The Ideation Process

Everyone has their own unique process for coming up with ideas. My goal is simply to document a repeatable process that I've found to work well. There may be times when you've solved the problem and came up with a brilliant solution as you're walking out of the client's office. But, those times are the rare exception. Most of the time you'll need to spend a significant amount of time working toward a solution.

## It Starts with Clearly Defining the Objective

Charles Kettering, the brilliant inventor, said, "A problem well stated is a problem half-solved." He was on to something. If we can't identify the problem, then how do we know what a good solution looks like? We have to understand the objective and goals if we're going to have a chance of coming up with a solution.

A well-defined problem will be specific and concrete. It will clearly outline the objective you're trying to accomplish. It should be realistic, actionable, and achievable. The more generic the problem, the harder coming up with a solution will be.

*We need to increase Q4 revenue* is an example of an objective that is too broad and generic to be actionable. Ideally you want something like: *Create a campaign that targets outdoor enthusiasts and drives tent sales by inspiring them to go camping.* The more concrete, realistic, and actionable you can define your objective, the easier it will be to solve the problem.

If you're struggling with defining the objective in a meaningful way, it can help to approach the business problem from the customer's point of view.

If you approach business problems from the standpoint of your own self-interest, then you ask questions like, *how do we increase our email sign-up rate by 50%?* The answers to these types of questions tend to be very tactical and limited in scope—things like pop-up ads and other annoying tactics that interrupt the user to try to force them to take an action. These approaches may help you reach your metric, but they sacrifice long-term brand value in favor of short-term gain. The business hits a metric, but the customer feels the pain.

However, if you take a more human-centered approach and ask the question from the customer's perspective, then the answer becomes much easier. For example, *What would make the email so irresistible that I would sign up if I had the chance?*

The answer to that question is much more likely to align the customer experience and business goals. It'll likely involve identifying a real pain point and solving the underlying reason for the low sign-up rate. If you succeed, it will be because you improved the customer experience, not because you tricked them.

## Give Yourself Time for Research and Inspiration

Research is a crucial part of the ideation process. Always allocate some time for research and inspiration. When possible, spend at least one full day doing research prior to concepting.

The goal is to go beyond the superficial aspects of the product and find out how the sausage is actually made. Take the factory tour (if there is one) and try to learn as much as possible about how the product is made. Look for little interesting tidbits of data. Read reviews, see what people love, and what they hate. Your goal at this point is just to digest as much information as possible.

Once you've learned all you can about the client's product, start to gather inspiration. Read the awards annuals (One Show, Comm Arts, etc.) and spend time checking out what's popular on the awards sites (AWWWards. com, theFWA.com, etc.). Check out other agencies and designers you respect.

Save the things you like even if they're not applicable. Your goal at this point is just to start assembling a pantry of potential ingredients that you can pull from later.

This is a step that a lot of people seem a little ashamed about. I always ask my students to show me their inspiration. Then something funny happens. They get nervous that I've asked to see the things that they've obviously modeled their work on. They don't realize that inspiration is an accepted part of the process. At the end of the day, all new ideas are just new expressions and interpretations of an idea that came before.

As a designer, if you don't see the ways in which other people have solved the problem, then you're trying to build something from scratch. All great things build upon the things that came before them. Don't be afraid of that. Embrace it.

That doesn't mean you can plagiarize. Your work still needs to be original, but it's ok to be influenced by something. That's the nature of inspiration.

## Creativity Is a Numbers Game

Every project starts the same way. A blank piece of paper stares you in the face. Distractions abound and somewhere there is a deadline looming. At this stage your only goal should be to come up with as many ideas and variations of ideas as you possibly can.

How many ideas are enough? There is never enough. Simply allocate an amount of time to spend: 1 hour, 2 hours, 8 hours, and try to come up with as many ideas as possible in that set period of time.

Defining a dedicated block of time for this task is important. The goal is to avoid interruptions and ignore all the potential distractions that are going to come your way.

A single interruption is all it takes to ruin your focus. You'll need another 25 minutes to return to the task and reach your previous level of performance (Thompson 2013).

For every 100 ideas you put down on paper, you'll have at least a few good ones. The secret is to keep pushing and never be satisfied with your initial efforts. The best ideas are always at the bottom of the list.

Start this process by coming up with a series of themes or buckets that you can explore. Try to come up with 10 general themes that you can explore.

These 10 themes could be something like:

1. Contests That Rely on User-Generated Content
2. Utilities or Tools That the Audience Would Find Useful
3. Cultural Issues I Could Take a Stand For
4. Cultural Issues I Could Take a Stand Against
5. Pranks I Could Play on the Unsuspecting Public
6. Symbols of Support That Would Let People Show Pride
7. Things This Client Could Do in the Real World That Would Make My Audience Smile/Laugh/Think/Cry
8. Things That Would Cause Controversy in the Industry
9. Celebrities That Could Be Utilized in Funny Ways
10. Offline Traditions I Could Translate Online in New Ways

Now choose a theme and come up with as many ideas as possible that fit that theme. It might be 10 ideas. It might be 25. At this point, it doesn't matter.

A word of warning—the first ideas you come up with will be bad. They always are. That's expected. Write them down and move on. As you work your way through this process you'll start to find some good ideas. Don't dwell on them. Just aim for volume at this point.

By the time all is said and done, you'll have somewhere between 50 and 100 ideas. Most of them won't be very good, but 10% will be solid.

Take that 10% and save them. Then get some sleep. You're probably exhausted.

## Why I Avoid Group Brainstorming

You may have noticed at this point that what I've described is a pretty solitary process.

In my experience, the initial stages of creativity are best handled as a solitary task. The classic group brainstorm simply doesn't work (Greenfield 2014). The social dynamics end up damaging the creative output.

One of the key issues is something called *collaboration fixation*. Due to our desire to conform, we end up fixating on other's ideas and mimicking them instead of exploring new avenues of thoughts. Therefore, the ideas generated during group brainstorming sessions often end up narrower and less creative (Kohn and Smith 2010).

If you try to group brainstorm your way to a solution, you're likely to get an idea that was created by the committee. It's best to avoid the group brainstorm altogether.

It's much better to have each member of your team ideate individually and then come together to review the best ideas that people have developed. I generally find the smaller the group the better. This group should have no more than five people. Two people works fine. It's better to have fewer people more focused on the task, than more people less focused.

## The Value of Letting Things Settle

Now that you've developed 5–10 pretty good initial ideas you can let things settle for a while. Walk away from the project for a day. Read a book, watch a documentary, and go for a long stroll. At this point in the process you want to let your unconscious do some of the heavy lifting. The goal is to stop trying so hard to come up with ideas. You've already primed the pump. Now it's time to just see if anything good bubbles up to the surface.

Most of the time during this phase of the process ideas will just start popping into your head. It might be while you're in the shower or when you're stuck in traffic. These little sudden flashes of insight are sometimes the best ideas of all. You may also find that an idea you loved yesterday no longer seems so great. That's ok too. Some ideas seem brilliant in the moment, but don't stay that way for very long.

## Narrowing Down Your Ideas

Now is the time to start narrowing and refining your concepts. If you're working with a small team, this is the perfect time to get everyone together to share ideas and give feedback.

The goal of sharing your ideas with the group is just to test the temperature. You're looking for two emotions: love and hate. Good ideas usually generate extreme responses. If you only get a tepid response, then you'll want to go back to the drawing board.

A good way to test if your idea has legs is to use a technique that Alex Bogusky at Crispin Porter + Bogusky developed. He required all ideas to be submitted in the form of a press release (DRT 2012). Instead of focusing on the execution of the idea, this approach allows you to focus on what aspect of the idea would actually get people talking.

Great ideas often generate earned media coverage. What would the newspaper headline about your idea say? If you can't figure it out, your idea may need some refinement.

You'll also want to start doing some research to make sure that your ideas are truly unique. If someone has already done that exact idea, then it's probably not worth pursuing.

## Pick Your Top Three and Create Concept Boards

So now it's time to get your ideas ready to share with the client. The best method I've found for this is a concept board. It's a simple approach that uses a description of the idea along with a reference visual.

Below are two example concepts boards. The goal of these is to get across the gist of the idea without going into too much detail. They also include just enough written information that the idea will be unlikely to get lost in translation (Figure 3.1).

**Founder Spikes**

Our goal is to craft a symbol of support that urban enthusiasts can display in their home or office.

Railroad spikes represent the heritage of the beltline. We'd source the spikes from local railroads and then add a design element such as paint and steel punching to increase attractiveness.

Each spike would be hand-numbered and be of a limited run to create a sense of scarcity.

**22.6-Mile Challenge**

We want to create a unique spin on the Walkathon—challenging enthusiasts to walk the entire beltline loop as part of the fund-raising effort and show of support.

Participants would have to raise at least $150 to enter.

Each person would get their own personalized fund-raising page that they could share on social media, allowing people to sponsor them on a per mile or one-time donation basis.

FIGURE 3.1    **Example concept boards for a fund-raising campaign.**

It really doesn't matter what form the concept board takes, as long as they get the general idea across. You can sketch them, create them in Photoshop, or make them in a presentation tool like the PowerPoint or Keynote.

## The Golden Rules of Giving Feedback

As your team grows, your role will shift from concepting ideas to guiding others in the ideation process. One skill every good creative director has is the ability to give great feedback. It's a crucial skill to develop if you want to be an effective leader. If you can't give good feedback, then you'll never be able to help others create their best work.

### Listen Carefully, and Ask Questions

The first step to providing good feedback is understanding the rationale behind the decisions that were made. *I don't like it* isn't good feedback. It's a personal preference disguised as feedback.

Focus on giving feedback that is nonopinionated and provides an opportunity for the person that created the work to provide context. A question like, *What's the thinking behind taking this approach?* will help you understand the reason the decisions were made so your input will be more informed and valuable.

### Start with the Nice

Try to accentuate the positive in the first part of your communication. If you always go straight into critiques/revisions, then the person you're working with will adopt a defensive stance. The result will be a combative conversation in which you'll be attacking and they'll be defending. You're on the same team and should act accordingly.

### Make It Actionable

The worst type of feedback you can give is nonactionable. *This isn't what I'm looking for* is the worst possible type of feedback. It gives no insight and provides no path forward. A better type of feedback would be, *I don't think option 1 works because it's not really aimed at our target audience. Option 2 has some potential, but try to explore a way to push the idea a little further and make it something people will talk about at the water cooler.*

## Be Completely Honest and Don't Pull Punches

The reason so much creative work is mediocre and even bad is that somewhere in the process of creation, the feedback became dishonest. You owe your team members honest feedback. It's the only way to set and maintain high creative standards. If it sucks, you have to say so.

This doesn't mean you have to be mean about it. Instead try to figure out the reason the work is off target. Did they just not spend enough time on it? Did they not do enough research? Or were they not sure of the objective? Figure out the root cause and give them a chance to fix it.

Telling someone that his or her work isn't up to the mark isn't easy, but if you're incapable of providing honest feedback, then you should let someone else lead.

On the other side of the coin, don't be the type of person that only criticizes and is never satisfied no matter how great the work really is. If the work is great, celebrate it. Tell the person you think it's awesome and that they're the wind beneath your wings.

Without good feedback, the people on your team will never reach their full potential. You owe it to your employees to provide the feedback they need to get better. They'll be happier and so will you.

## References

DRT. September 20, 2012. Alex Bogusky interview. http://drt.fm/alex-bogusky/#!/ transcript. Accessed on January 28, 2016.

Greenfield, R. July 29, 2014. Brainstorming doesn't work: Try this instead. *Fast Company*. http://www.fastcompany.com/3033567/agendas/brainstorming-doesnt-work-try-this-technique-instead. Accessed on January 28, 2016.

Kohn, N. W. and Smith, S. M. 2010. Collaborative fixation: Effects of others' ideas on brainstorming. *Applied Cognitive Psychology* 25:359–371.

Sullivan, L. 1998. *Hey Whipple, Squeeze This*. John Wiley & Sons, Hoboken, NJ.

Thompson, H. and Sullivan, B. May 05, 2013. A focus on distraction. *New York Times*. http://www.nytimes.com/2013/05/05/opinion/sunday/a-focus-on-distraction.html?_r=0. Accessed on January 28, 2016.

Wiesel, E. October 27, 1986. *US News & World Report*. http://wist.info/wiesel-elie/8151/. Accessed on April 19, 2016.

# Chapter 4

# The Elements
# of Great Design

*Out of clutter find simplicity. From discord find harmony.*

***Albert Einstein***

## What Is Great Design?

This question seems like it should be easy to answer. The difficulty lies in the fact that design is in and of itself a difficult thing to define. Design is a process, but it's also an outcome or result.

So let's take the highest-level definition of design: that design is the act of solving a problem—and break it down from there. Based on this definition, for a design to be great, it first must solve some sort of problem. That problem could be functional, it could be visual, or it could be experiential.

If design doesn't solve a problem—then it's not design. It's self-expression. It's art. In this chapter, we'll review the key elements of great design and show how they can be applied through examples.

## Great Design Is Intuitive

The next attribute of great design is that it is intuitive and easy to understand. When people say that great design is simple, what they really mean is that it feels simple.

This is especially true of digital experiences. The reason that human-centered design has become so important is that digital interfaces are less self-evident than their mechanical counterparts. Mechanical devices generally have a form that gives a clue to their operation. A knob on a stereo looks twistable, while a curtain cord looks pullable, and the ways in which gears interact can be figured out through simple observation alone.

But digital interfaces are more abstract than their physical counterparts. It is only through the on-screen interface that it's usability can be derived. Their blank physical appearance doesn't give clue to their intentions.

Great design in the digital world overcomes these challenges and feels intuitive, elegant, and simple. It does this by understanding the user's goals, providing simple paths for the user to follow, and establishes a consistent set of patterns and interactions that the user uses throughout the experience.

For example, let's look at the way that Uber simplified the act of ordering car service.

Traditionally when ordering a car service, you have to provide certain information. The address where you want to be picked up, the time at which you want the driver to arrive, and the method of payment you'd like to use (see Figure 4.1).

This is a lot of information. To overcome this complexity, Uber makes a number of assumptions. It assumes that the location you're at is where you want to be picked up. It also assumes that you need to be picked up at this very moment, not in the future, and that the payment method you used last time is the same payment method you used this time.

Instead of spending 45 seconds filling out your information, they've made the experience frictionless. You simply open the app, click a single button, and you're done (see Figure 4.2).

This requires more complexity behind the scenes, but lowers the level of complexity for the user.

Rarely is great design truly simple. It's usually complex, but it feels so intuitive that we perceive it to be simple.

Dieter Rams (2016), the great industrial designer said, "Good design … clarifies the product's structure. Better still, it can make the product talk. At best, it is self-explanatory." This is as true for digital experience as it is for physical objects. Great design shouldn't require a set of instructions.

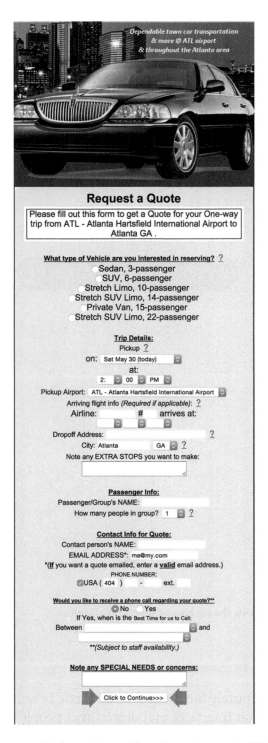

**FIGURE 4.1    The amount of information you'd need to enter on a traditional car service website is overwhelming.**

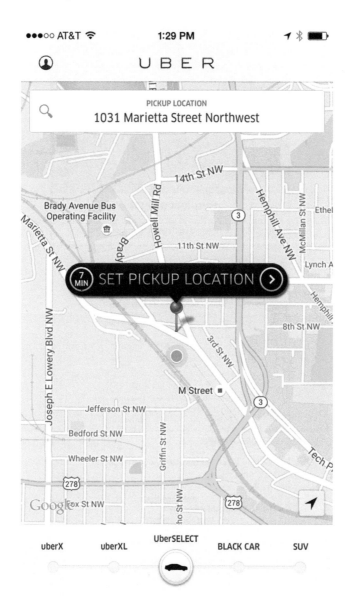

FIGURE 4.2   **Uber made the car request process frictionless.**

## Great Design Is Aesthetically Pleasing

Great design isn't purely functional. It's aesthetic as well. Research has consistently shown that interfaces and objects that people rate as aesthetically pleasing are also perceived to work better (Norman 2002).

Even if they contain the exact same information, users will rate a well-designed interface as more usable and pleasing every single time simply because it's more pleasing to the eye.

A group of nineteenth century craftsmen called *the Shakers* expressed this elegantly in a proverb about their design philosophy.

> Don't make something unless it is both necessary and useful; but if it is both necessary and useful, don't hesitate to make it beautiful.

**Shaker Proverb**

Some companies take pride in their lack of design. Craigslist is a great example. But it has the advantage of incumbency and network effects that come from being the first market leader. To say its success is related to its lack of design isn't accurate.

This doesn't mean that you should go overboard with ornamentation and facade, but it's also wise to avoid the sheer brutalism that sometimes results from too much reliance on the idea that form must always follow function. There are many paths toward beauty.

## Great Design Avoids Cliché

Another way to say this is *don't be a hack*. Every industry has its visual clichés. They've been used and abused. The woman smiling while eating salad or the guy in the datacenter with his arms crossed.

I remember reading a technology magazine a few years ago, and we counted the same stock image of a female in a datacenter in two different ads for two different companies in the same industry. Now some would say their problem was that they didn't purchase a rights-managed image. I would argue their problem was that their thinking was so unoriginal that they chose the same cliché image as their competitor (Figure 4.3).

FIGURE 4.3    **Avoid images like this at all costs.**

Great design avoids this. It finds ways to upend the category and be unique in its visual approach and expression. That uniqueness is what allows it to get noticed and stand out in a crowd of sameness. Great design is unique in form and expression.

## Great Design Is Aimed at a Specific Audience

Recently, while speaking at a conference, someone asked me what to do when *everyone* is your target audience. I responded that by definition, if everyone is your audience then you don't have a target audience.

Great design is always aimed at a specific audience. From that focus it derives its power. Now that doesn't mean you have to craft your design to the needs of a specific demographic. Despite the confusion of way too many marketers, target audience and demographic are not the same thing. A 55-year black female isn't a target audience. It's a demographic description.

Recently, we were engaged by the Atlanta BeltLine to launch its first ever grassroots fundraising campaign. The BeltLine is an ambitious project to turn 22 miles of old railroad tracks into a series of parks and transit that will transform Atlanta (Brown 2014).

This audience was defined not by demographics, but instead by worldview. We decided to create something that would reach the urban enthusiasts. People who cared about walkability, who took pride in this city, and were excited about the Atlanta BeltLine's potential for transforming the region.

Since this was a grassroots campaign, we knew that a simple call for donations would fall on deaf ears. The idea would need to be able to spread via word of mouth and earned media.

It turned out the answer to our challenge required us to look toward the Atlanta BeltLine's past. When construction on the BeltLine started, it saved the old railroad tracks that once lined the paths. Those rails were a piece of history that we thought people would want to own.

So we created a limited edition symbol of support using these old rails. Working with a local blacksmith we crafted 1000 limited edition slices of history. Each hand-stamped with the BeltLine logo and available for purchase online. It was designed to be a symbol of support for a project that people loved (Figure 4.4).

In less than three weeks after the launch, we sold enough of these slices of rail to blow the original $40,000 fundraising goal out of the water. This was all accomplished without a single dollar spent on media or advertising.

Instead of demographics—great design targets an audience based on their goals, worldviews, and desires.

**FIGURE 4.4    Website for the Build the BeltLine campaign.**

## Great Design Speaks to the Heart and Changes Minds

Design is an expressive medium. It can evoke an emotional response from the audience. It can be calming and reassuring, it can make you laugh, or it can make you angry. If you're designing without considering the emotional component, then you're not utilizing design to its fullest power.

The best designers understand this. They realize that design has the ability to communicate and sometimes even persuade. The goal isn't emotional manipulation—it's emotional truth. Great design finds a universal truth about the human experience and communicates it in a way that speaks directly to your heart and mind.

A great example is from the apparel brand Guy Cotten. It sells outdoor gear and lifejackets for sailors and fishermen. It created a website called *Sortie En Mer* (https://SortienMer.com) that tells the story of a person drowning after falling off of a boat while not wearing a life jacket (Sortie En Mer 2014). But what made the experience engaging and memorable was that it was interactive. In order to try to stay afloat, the user must continually scroll to avoid drowning. It effectively simulates the helplessness of drowning (Figure 4.5).

Once you finally succumb, you're presented with a simple message: "At sea, you tire faster than you think. Whenever you go out to sea, wear your life jacket" (Sortie En Mer 2014).

It's a message that anyone who visited the website is likely to remember for a long time.

FIGURE 4.5    **Keep scrolling or else you'll drown.**

## Great Design Sweats the Details

Charles Eames said, "The details are not the details. The details are the design." What he meant by this was that great design is polished and elegant. The details are as considered as the big picture concept.

Think about your favorite digital experiences. What little details do you love? It may be the .gif animation of a digital high five that MailChimp gives you after you send an e-mail campaign (Figure 4.6). It might be the fact that Google Chrome automatically translates pages that are in another language.

Dan Saffer calls these *microinteractions* (Saffer 2012). It is these interactions that generally only serve a single use case that can make the difference between a good experience and a great one.

FIGURE 4.6    **MailChimp's delightful animated high five.**

FIGURE 4.7   **AirBNB goes in depth on a Buenos Aires neighborhood.**

The difference between a great experience and a good experience is attention to the details that are normally overlooked. Attention to detail and improving these small moments of potential delight are what separate a good experience from a great one.

## Great Design Requires Great Content

A great wrapper on the outside can't make up for a lack of compelling content on the inside. It's as true for books and websites as it is for people. An attractive package with bad content on the inside is empty calories. It's pure sugar. After the rush, nothing worthwhile remains.

Great design is informed by great content. This is what gives it meaning and purpose. Design without content is simply a decorative facade.

AirBNB is a great example. Their city guides are not only well-designed, but provide valuable information to prospective travelers looking to decide where to stay. They give you information on cities and the neighborhoods within them so that as a traveler, if you are looking to book an apartment/house, you can make an informed decision (Figure 4.7).

You may think that content strategy is someone else's job, but it's not. You own the digital experience and it's up to you to make sure that the content is as carefully considered as the interface.

## Great Design Is Timeless

When done well, design is timeless in nature. It doesn't adhere to fads and sacrifice trendiness for functionality. The works of Phillip Johnson, Mies

Van De Rohe, and Dieter Rams feel as modern today as they did when they were created. They're timeless in nature.

In today's digital-focused world, design trends come and go quickly. There is no right answer to the question of whether one trend is better than the other.

*Great design doesn't expire. It becomes iconic.*

## References

Brown, R. February 15, 2014. Beltline provides new life to railroad tracks. *The New York Times.* http://www.nytimes.com/2013/02/15/us/beltline-provides-new-life-to-railroad-tracks-in-atlanta.html. Accessed on January 28, 2016.

Norman, D. A. April 1, 2002. Emotion & design: Attractive things work better. http://www.jnd.org/dn.mss/emotion_design_at.html. Accessed on January 28, 2016.

Rams, D. 2016. Ten principles for good design. *About Vitsœ-Good Design-Vitsœ.* https://www.vitsoe.com/rw/about/good-design. Accessed on April 18, 2016.

Saffer, D. November 17, 2012. About the book: Microinteractions. http://microinteractions.com/what-is-a-microinteraction/. Accessed on January 28, 2016.

Sortie En Mar. 2014. *Sortie En Mer.* https://SortienMer.com. Accessed on January 1, 2015.

# Chapter 5

# Changing Behavior by Design

*Rigid, the skeleton of habit alone upholds the human frame.*

*Virginia Woolf*
(Mrs. Dalloway, *1925*)

## Designing to Drive Behavior and Build Habits

We've already established that design is about problem solving and many of the most difficult problems that you'll face will be around encouraging your audience to take a desired action.

In this chapter, we'll talk about the process of designing for behavior change, the core elements of human behavior and why they're important, review some practical persuasion techniques that will help you create more effective campaigns and methods you can use to help turn actions into habits.

## Humans Are an Operating System Loaded with Bugs

Our understanding of human behavior has changed dramatically over the years. Our original understanding was based on early economic models first developed in the mid-1800s. These ideas, such as Adam Smith's Invisible

Hand Theory and Jeremy Bentham's Theory of Utilitarianism led to the creation of what is now referred to as the *rational actor* model of human behavior.

This model posits that humans seek to maximize personal advantage. Weighing costs against benefits and then selecting for best outcome. In this conception of humanity, we're essentially an operating system that behaves predictably and rationally.

But we now know that's not the whole story. Modern social scientists have identified more than 100 unique biases in human behavior that lead us to behave irrationally (Wikipedia 2016).

These inherent human biases are the reason that we're more scared of sharks than falling coconuts, even though coconuts kill more people each and every year (Onion 2002). They're also the reason that we play slot machines even though we know the odds aren't in our favor.

## Facts Are Not Enough to Change Behavior

Since we're irrational, simple facts alone aren't enough to change behavior. We only wish it was that easy. If facts alone were enough, then the Surgeon General's warning about the link between cigarettes and cancer would've stopped people from smoking when it was first issued in 1966. Instead, cigarette consumption actually peaked in the United States in 1981—15 years after the warning was issued (American Lung Association 2011).

This is because once we choose a belief system; we don't accept evidence that challenges that belief. The more evidence we gather, the more hardened our beliefs become.

Scientists who study this call it: *the Cultural Cognition of Risk*. The more knowledge people have, the more their existing beliefs are strengthened (Cultural Cognition Project at Yale Law School 2008).

A recent study conducted by the Cultural Cognition project researchers found that ordinary members of the public do not become more concerned about climate change as their science comprehension increases. Instead, the degree of polarization among cultural groups with opposing beliefs increases. The more scientific evidence people that deny climate change is real are shown that they are wrong, the stronger they believe that they're right (Kahan et al. 2012).

There's nothing people hate more than being told they're wrong, even if it's true. If you have to change someone's beliefs to get him or her to take action then you're in for a tough road. No matter what evidence you provide, it will merely reinforce their existing belief. Instead you have to take a different approach.

## You Have to Framing Your Argument in a Way That Fits in Their Existing Worldview

Telling your Rush Limbaugh-loving Uncle that he needs to watch that great Al Gore climate change movie isn't going to work.

In his worldview, Al Gore is the guy who lied about inventing the Internet and climate change is just a hoax. The simple fact is: The argument that convinced you is unlikely to convince them.

However, if his friend starts talking about the need to protect God's gift and how pollution from the local coal plant is causing acid rain that's killing the forest he hunts in every Saturday, then he just might listen.

If you can frame your message in a way that fits into his worldview, then persuasion is possible. If not, your argument will backfire.

## The Three Core Elements of Human Behavior

Dr. B.J. Fogg, a professor at Stanford University who studies human behavior, says that there are three basic elements to human behavior. For any behavior to take place, these three items must be present and the level of motivation must be greater than the level of difficulty required by the task you're asking a person to complete.

Mapped out as an equation, it looks something like this (see Figure 5.1):

$$Behavior = Motivation + Ability + Trigger.$$

He calls this the Fogg Model of Human Behavior and it's a helpful tool to visualize whether or not a behavior is likely to take place (Fogg 2009).

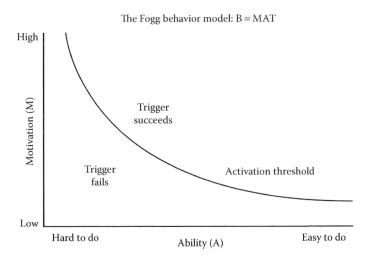

**FIGURE 5.1    Dr. B.J. Fogg's Model of Human Behavior.**

- *Motivation*: Motivation is simply the desire you have to do something. If people are more motivated, then they're more likely to take an action.
- *Ability*: How easy or difficult a task is to complete. The harder the task, the more motivation it will require to trigger a behavior.
- *Trigger*: A call to action that causes us to act. It could be explicit like a reminder that pops up on your phone, or less obvious like seeing a bag of chips on the table triggering you to snack.

## How to Increase Motivation in an Irrational Being?

There are two core types of motivation.

1. *Extrinsic motivation*: External motivators, such as desire for rewards or to avoid punishment. If you want to increase the level of extrinsic motivation, just make the reward higher or the punishment more intense.
2. *Intrinsic motivation*: These are internal motivators that come from trying to enhance your sense of self-concept. The result must be one that helps the person to be seen as the type of person they desire to be. If you want to increase the level of intrinsic motivation, then you have to design experiences that allow for people to have a sense of autonomy, mastery, and purpose.

When crafting experiences, you have to think carefully about what type of motivation you're trying to build. While extrinsic motivations may seem like the easiest route to success, they do have some disadvantages.

Daniel Pink (2009) in his book, *Drive: The Surprising Truth About What Motivates Us*, points out one of the potential issues with relying too heavily on extrinsic rewards:

> The problem with making an extrinsic reward the only destination that matters is that some people will choose the quickest route there, even if it means taking the low road. Indeed, most of the scandals and misbehavior that have seemed endemic to modern life involve shortcuts.

Another potential issue is that using tangible rewards to increase extrinsic motivation can actually cause a reduction in intrinsic motivation. The reason is simple. Cooking a delicious meal for my family is a hobby that I take pride in. Cooking a delicious meal for money feels like a job.

So instead of relying heavily on tangible extrinsic rewards to increase motivation, find ways that you can help people build intrinsic motivation. Create experiences that have a clear purpose and help them tell a story to the wider world about the type of person they are.

Instead of relying on tangible rewards, help them reap intangible rewards by tapping into their basic human desires.

## Our Basic Human Desires

All of us have at our core basic human desires that we're motivated to try and fulfill. It could be that we're seeking social status or love. These are powerful motivators that don't necessarily rely on tangible rewards (Grabmeier 2000).

- Physical activity
- Power
- Romance
- Collecting
- Social contact
- Social status
- Tranquility
- Vengeance
- Acceptance
- Curiosity
- Eating
- Family
- Honor
- Idealism
- Independence
- Order

You see this all the time in marketing. Luxury goods try to speak to your desire for social status. Life insurance companies try to speak to your desire to protect your family after you're gone.

When we were working on a campaign for a well-known island resort designed to entice brides-to-be to get married there, we developed two messages for testing. One was a discount offer (book three nights, get the fourth free). The other was focused on the timeless themes of romance and tranquility. The desire for romance and tranquility outperformed the simple discount offer by almost 80%.

By understanding these basic desires, you can look for opportunities to more effectively engage your target audience.

## If You Can't Change the Actual Experience, Change the Perception

Whenever possible, you want to change the experience to make the task easier. But there will be times when you can't actually change the experience.

If you're redesigning an online form that collects data for a health insurance provider, no matter how many times you ask to simplify the insurance form, it's unlikely that they'll be willing to change it.

So how do you improve the experience without changing the reality of its performance? You focus on the perception of its performance.

Expensive wine tastes better. Not because it is better, but because it's perceived to be better. Price is a signaling mechanism. In general, we believe that if something is more expensive, then it must be better.

Robin Goldstein from the American Association of Wine Economists conducted a well-known study where they did blind taste tests of expensive wines. Their findings show that if people don't know the price of an expensive wine, then they don't enjoy it any more than other less expensive wines. In other words, the enjoyment of an expensive wine comes not from its taste, but from the fact you know it's expensive (Goldstein et al. 2008).

This has some interesting implications for experience design.

Imagine two hours spent drinking wine with friends. Now imagine two hours spent on a plane flying from Atlanta to New York. The reality is that the amount of time is the same, but the time spent flying is going to be perceived much differently.

To keep flyers from becoming impatient or irritated, the engineering approach says to find ways to bring the flight time down. But it could cost billions of dollars to research and develop new technology to speed up commercial planes when it would likely be more effective to focus on making the in-flight experience more enjoyable so it's perceived to go faster.

Some people may claim that this is trickery, but it's not. Our perception is our reality. Feeling faster is as good as being faster.

You can apply this to digital design by breaking large, difficult processes into smaller steps and using progressive disclosure to make complex processes feel simpler than they really are.

Sometimes simply changing the perception of an experience is as good as changing the experience itself.

## Create Triggers That Are Actionable, Noticeable, and Timely

Triggers are simply things that remind us to take an action, but not all triggers are created equally. There are three key things that a trigger needs to be effective. It must be actionable, noticeable, and timely.

First, the trigger has to be concrete and actionable. It has to be clear in what it's asking us to do and point to a specific action. If you set a calendar reminder each morning that told you to get in shape—it's unlikely that you would actually go work out. It's not specific enough. It doesn't point you to a specific action.

If instead, you set a calendar reminder to run for 20 minutes. Then you'll have much better response rate. It's actionable. It points to a specific action.

The second thing that an effective trigger must be is noticeable. It's common sense. If you're alarm is on silent, you're not going to wake up. If someone can't find the button to take the action you want him or her to take, they're not going to click it.

The third thing that separates good triggers from bad ones is that good triggers are timely. They occur when we are motivated and able to perform the behavior.

The ancient Greeks called this moment *kairos*—meaning the right or opportune moment for a certain thing to happen or for the truth to emerge. It's that perfect meeting of motivation and ability where it becomes possible to get someone to take action.

It's almost like dating. You can't try to kiss someone when you've only known them five minutes. It'll backfire. The same holds true for experience design. If you try to trigger a behavior too soon, then you're risking alienating the audience.

## Five Methods of Persuasion That Can Help Drive Behaviors

When you think of the art of persuasion, you probably think of a sales person trying to convince someone to buy something, or a politician trying to get elected. But the art of persuasion applies as much to experience design as it does to person-to-person interaction.

Robert Cialdini first outlined these principles in his book *Influence: The Psychology of Persuasion* (Cialdini 2007). These methods can be used to create a sense of urgency, act as proof points, and increase the motivation level of the audience you're trying to reach.

### Use Reciprocity to Create a Sense of Obligation

The first principle is called *reciprocity*. The idea is that when a person or organization provides us with something, then we attempt to repay him or her in kind.

Reciprocation produces a sense of obligation. This sense of obligation makes someone more likely to take a desired action.

This is why promoters working the streets of large cities hand out flyers. It's not because they expect you to keep the flyer. Instead, it's the fact that if you accept the flyer, you'll become much more likely to listen to their pitch.

In the digital realm, this same approach applies. If you're producing really valuable content like a detailed report, then don't require people to fill out a form to access the full report. Instead give a bit before taking. Create an article highlighting the key points of the report and then allow the user to download the full report if they find the article interesting.

## Use Commitment to Create a Tendency for People to Follow Through

Once a person actively commits to a cause or belief—no matter how small the initial commitment is—they are likely to consistently follow through on that commitment.

A great example comes from research done by a group of Israeli scientists in 1983. Researchers asked half an apartment complex to sign a petition supporting for the construction of a recreation center for the handicapped. Two weeks later, the researchers returned. This time, they asked all residents, even those who they had not asked to sign the petition, to donate money toward the center.

According to the study, among the residents who had been previously asked to sign the petition supporting the center, the donation rate was a staggering 92% compared to just above 50% among those who had not been previously asked to sign the petition (Cialdini 2001).

Learn from this approach. Ask users to make a small commitment prior to making a large one. Once you get your foot in the door, then guide them down the path to take a larger step.

## Use Social Proof to Drive Behavior Change

Social proof is similar to peer pressure. It's the idea that people are influenced when the behavior of their peers is made visible/apparent. It's the reason that we think a nightclub with a long line out front is better than the one with no line. We assume the people who are waiting in line are more informed than we are, and are waiting for good reason.

It's also why we're more likely to purchase products and services from the market leader. If 10 million people enjoyed something, then it's likely that I will too.

A San Francisco Bay Area water utility system used this principle to reduce water consumption.

When a user logs in to view their bill, they're shown how their water consumption compares with their neighbors. They're rated *Great, Good, or Take Action*, depending on the results.

Most people don't want to be outliers. If their consumption is higher then their neighbors, they become more likely to reduce their usage. By making this fact visible, you can drive changes in their behavior.

This simple approach resulted in a 5% reduction in water consumption (Boxall 2014).

## Use Authority to Provide Credibility

We have the tendency to believe that if an expert says something, then it must be true. People like to listen to those who they believe are knowledgeable and trustworthy.

As a marketer, you're seen as biased and untrustworthy. Half of the Americans (50%) don't trust what they see, read, and hear in advertisements. About 44% think that advertisements are dishonest (YouGov PLC 2014).

However, if the media delivers your message, or if a trusted key influencer talks about your product/service, then people are more likely to believe it. These third-party endorsements make your message more effective.

A recent Nielsen study backs this up. The study finds that 85% of consumers look to content from experts before they make a purchasing decision and 67% of consumers said an endorsement from an unbiased expert would make them more likely to purchase a product (Nielsen 2013).

If you have credible endorsements from authority, showcase them.

## Use Scarcity to Create Value

Earlier we talked about the fact that people believe that price derives from value, but that's not true. Price is a signaling mechanism of value. If something is more expensive, we assume it's better. The same holds for scarcity. If something is rare, we want it more. It creates a sense of urgency and desire.

Scarcity doesn't only derive from limited numbers. It also derives from limiting the time of availability. The McRib is a cult food product only because it's availability is limited. People build locators for it, they light up twitter when it comes back, and it flies off the shelf each time it makes an appearance. However, if it were always available, this wouldn't happen. It only happens due to artificial scarcity.

We used this principle as a cornerstone of a campaign we created to preserve a landmark piece of architecture called the Eames House. The house was designed by Ray & Charles Eames who were legends of modern American design. It served as their home and studio for the most prolific part of their lives and the foundation that managed it needed to raise $150,000 to help fund it's preservation.

As part of the campaign, we created and sold a series of prints that would appeal to the design enthusiast who wanted to help preserve the Eames legacy. The final products were a set of original works inspired by the elegant geometry and understated simplicity of Eames designs. Each piece was a simple offset print with blank emboss, printed on a special Eames paper (Figure 5.2).

FIGURE 5.2    **The Eames House limited edition prints.**

To create a sense of scarcity, we limited the production run to only 750 prints. Once they were sold out, then they were done. All prints were hand numbered to make them feel more special. The prints were offered for sale directly to the public, with all funds being directed toward the Eames foundation.

The result was astounding. In just a few weeks, the campaign raised in excess of $250,000 and garnered coverage in major publications like *USA Today* and *The LA Times*.

By creating a sense of scarcity around the prints and tying it to a worthy cause, we were able to drive demand.

## Engineer Variable Rewards and Repetition to Build Habits

So now that we've talked about designing to drive behaviors, let's talk a little bit about what it takes to turn a behavior into a habit.

Once you're able to trigger a behavior, there are only two additional factors that you need to build a habit: variable rewards and repetition over time.

### Use Variable Rewards to Drive Engagement

What do we mean by variable reward? Variable rewards are simply rewards that are delivered unpredictably based on an action.

The classic example of the variable reward is the slot machine. They are engineered to be addictive. You don't win every single time, but you win just enough to keep you wanting more. The next coin you play could win the jackpot so keep playing.

These variable rewards are why slot machines are so effective and players are often reluctant to quit.

But variable rewards aren't just used to create gambling addicts. These same principles can be applied to encouraging positive behaviors.

Peter Tufano, a former professor at the Harvard Business School, developed a savings program for local credit unions that took what people loved about lotteries (the variable reward) and turned it into a way to encourage people to deposit money in their savings account.

Each $25 deposit gives the depositor an entry into the prize-winning raffle.

The program, called *Save To Win*, was launched in Michigan and was a resounding success. By the end of 2012, there were more than 40,000 Save To Win account holders and more than $72,000,000 was deposited. Most amazingly, 56% of those who opened an account were classified as *nonsavers* meaning that they reported that they were not regular savers before opening their Save to Win account (Doorways to Dreams Fund 2013).

Variable rewards don't just have to be tangible things like money. They can rely on our intrinsic desires as motivators to drive behavior.

In fact, gamification guru Gabe Zichermann's research leads him to believe that tangible rewards like cash aren't always the most effective rewards for people looking to drive behavior. Instead, he recommends using on what he calls the SAPS rewards model (NPR Staff 2011).

## The SAPS Rewards Model

So let's look at Gabe Zichermann's reward model a little bit closer. This model is designed reflect our intrinsic desires. These rewards, listed in order of effectiveness, can be used to build loyalty and drive long-term behavior in a brand's products & services.

- *Status*: We all yearn to feel important. Rewards that allow users to advance their status within their peer group are a great way to provide incentive for participation. Reddit and their use of *Karma* to indicate how much good a user has done within the community is a great example of a status-based reward system. For each post a user makes on Reddit they get karma points based on how much other users like the post. Karma is prominently displayed next to their username as an indicator of status within the community
- *Access*: The desire to be a part of something exclusive is powerful. Access is a way to reward users with exclusive offers. Political

campaigns are masters of this. They setup special campaign briefing conference calls for big supporters, and hold private/exclusive fund-raisers for their large donors as way to reward them and encourage further involvement

- *Power*: Users who are given power and responsibility feel a sense of ownership and empowerment. Whether it's the ability to invite a friend to an exclusive system, or a position as a moderator—these actions fulfill our desire for influence and control. This is why closed betas that rely on invites work so well. Those that already have access to the system feel like they have the power to grant access to those they deem worthy
- *Stuff*: Stuff is simply tangible rewards like money, gifts and other freebies. While tangible rewards can be great motivators, the cost makes them less effective in sustaining long-term behavior in the digital realm. However, if you can create a sense of scarcity around items then the value of the item to the user can far outweigh the cost and it becomes more useful as a tool.

## Build Repetition through Feedback Loops

We've explored how the variable rewards help in creating habits, but we're still missing a key ingredient. That ingredient is repetition. Without repetition habit-formation just won't happen.

If you want to create something that becomes a part of people's daily existence then you're going to need strong feedback loops. In fact, most successful apps like Facebook, Instagram and Twitter rely heavily on very similar feedback loops as a key part of their success.

## The Power of Positive Network Effects

The biggest feedback loop that powers these apps is the positive network effect that results from the fact that each new user makes the platform itself more valuable. Each new member contributes new content for people to consume and adds a new person for others to interact with.

These positive network effects create a feedback loop that creates an incentive for existing users to try to get new users to join as the experience for all users improves as new users are added. This leads to viral growth and rapid adoption.

## The New and Potentially Compelling the Content Feedback Loop

Every time you open one of the successful social apps we discussed above you're presented with new, relevant content. This isn't by accident. They realize that by showing you something new and potentially compelling each time you open the app, they are basically building a variable reward system. You open the app every few hours to check for new content just to ensure that you're not missing out on something compelling. It's the digital content version of a slot machine.

## The Variable Reward for Contribution Feedback Loop

You'll also notice that most major social apps today rely on user contributions for content. For contributors to stay engaged you have to find a way to reward them. This is where the contribution feedback loop comes in.

Every time a user posts a photo, a tweet or updates their status there is a variable reward mechanism that gives them status. The names for these rewards all differ: likes, comments, retweets, favorites—but at their core they all work the same. They encourage the user to come back to check to see if anyone has responded to their contribution or given them positive feedback. The result is that users who contribute feel positive about their efforts and are more likely to contribute in the future.

## How Long Does It Take to Build Habits?

Now that we've talked about some of the ways in which you encourage the formation of habits you're probably asking how long does it take? The answer is: it depends.

If you're trying to get in the habit of drinking a glass of water in the morning, then it could take as little as 20 days to form a habit. If you're trying to do 50 sit-ups before breakfast, then it will likely take more than 100 days for it to become automatic (Dean 2009).

Much like motivation must be equal to the difficulty of the task when trying to trigger a behavior. The amount of time it takes to form a habit also depends on the difficulty of the task at hand. The harder the task, the longer habit formation will take.

## References

American Lung Association. July 1, 2011. Trends in tobacco use. http://www.lung.org/finding-cures/our-research/trend-reports/Tobacco-Trend-Report.pdf. Accessed on January 2, 2016.

Boxall, B. March 03, 2014. *LA Times*. http://articles.latimes.com/2014/mar/03/science/la-sci-sn-behavioral-water-efficiency-20140303. Accessed on January 28, 2016.

Cialdini, R. October 01, 2001. Harvard business review: Harnessing the science of persuasion. *Harvard Business Review*. http://hbr.org/2001/10/harnessing-the-science-of-persuasion/ar/3. Accessed on January 28, 2016.

Cialdini, R. B. 2007. *Influence: The Psychology of Persuasion*. Collins, New York.

Cultural Cognition Project at Yale Law School. April 21, 2008. Homepage. http://www.culturalcognition.net/browse-papers/cultural-cognition-as-a-conception-of-the-cultural-theory-of.html. Accessed on January 28, 2016.

Dean, J. September 21, 2009. PSYblog. http://www.spring.org.uk/2009/09/how-long-to-form-a-habit.php. Accessed on January 28, 2016.

Doorways to Dreams Fund. July 01, 2013. Save to win: Highlights from Michigan 2012. http://www.d2dfund.org/files/2012%20PLS%20MI%20Highlight%20Reel_0.pdf. Accessed on January 28, 2016.

Fogg, B.J. March 22, 2009. BJ Fogg behavior model. http://www.behaviormodel.org/. Accessed on January 28, 2016.

Goldstein, R., Almenberg, J., Dreber, A., Emerson, J. W., Herschkowitsch, A. and Katz, J. 2008. Do more expensive wines taste better? Evidence from a large sample of blind tastings. *AAWE Working Paper No. 16*.

Grabmeier, J. June 28, 2000. New theory of motivation lists 16 basic desires that guide us. *Ohio State University Research News*. http://researchnews.osu.edu/archive/whoami.htm. Accessed on January 28, 2016.

Kahan, D. M., Peters, E., Wittlin, M., Slovic, P., Ouellette, L. L., Braman, D. and Mandel, G. May 27, 2012. The polarizing impact of science literacy and numeracy on perceived climate change risks. *Nature*. http://www.nature.com/nclimate/journal/v2/n10/full/nclimate1547.html. Accessed on January 28, 2016.

Nielsen. September 17, 2013. Under the influence: Consumer trust in advertising. http://www.nielsen.com/us/en/insights/news/2013/under-the-influence-consumer-trust-in-advertising.html. Accessed on April 18, 2016.

NPR Staff. March 27, 2011. NPR. http://www.npr.org/2011/03/27/134866003/gamifying-the-system-to-create-better-behavior. Accessed on January 28, 2016.

Onion, A. May 21, 2002. *ABC News*. http://abcnews.go.com/Technology/story?id=97993. Accessed on January 28, 2016.

Pink, D. H. 2009. *Drive: The Surprising Truth About What Motivates Us*. Riverhead, New York.

Wikipedia. January 25, 2016. List of cognitive biases. http://en.wikipedia.org/wiki/List_of_cognitive_biases. Last Modified on May 22, 2016.

Woolf, V. 1925. *Mrs. Dalloway*. Brace and Co., Harcourt, New York.

YouGov PLC. April 08, 2014. YouGov research. http://research.yougov.com/news/2014/04/08/truth-advertising-50-dont-trust-what-they-see-read/. Accessed on January 28, 2016.

# Chapter 6

# Designing Content That's Awesome

*Content informs design; design without content is decoration.*

**Jeffrey Zeldman**
(A Design Apart Q&A, *2009*)

The difference between a great digital experience and a mediocre one generally boils down to one word: content.

Content isn't just copy and images. It's video, animation, infographics, interactive widgets, and tools.

If you come from a design background, the idea of being responsible for a site's content can be a bit intimidating. But you don't need to be a copywriter. You just need to be able to conceptualize and produce content that your target audience will love.

In this chapter, we'll talk about how to approach content strategy to ensure what you're producing is awesome, the importance of storytelling, what Walt Disney can teach you about experience design; advice on producing specific types of content such as video, animation, and infographics; and how to find and work with production partners to bring your content to life.

## Content Is Eating the World

Seth Godin said, "Content marketing is the only marketing left" (Leslie 2015). By the looks of my inbox, my Facebook feed and every other social channel I subscribe to, every marketer in the world agrees with him and they're all fighting for my attention.

So if everybody understands the importance of content, why is so much of it bad? It's because most marketers create content that tries to sell the audience instead of helping them. This leads to useless white papers, terrible videos, and other content atrocities.

## Make It Useful Or Make It Entertaining

A good rule of thumb is that content should do one of two things. It should be useful or it should be entertaining. If it's neither, then it doesn't need to be created.

## Designing Content That Is Useful

So how do you know what your audience will find useful? Start by going back to your customer research.

Take the buyer journey map you built earlier and then start mapping content to each phase.

Think about the questions the audience is asking throughout the buyer journey. Can you create content that helps them answer those questions before they purchase, or overcome potential hurdles or objections that they might have? After they've purchased, how can you help them make the most of what they have bought?

Remember that content isn't just the written word. So try to find ways to use interactivity to enhance the experience and make it something more unique than just words on a screen.

A few years ago, my agency was working with a solar panel manufacturer called MAGE Solar. They were just launching their U.S. operations and they contracted with us to redesign their main website.

Based on our research, we knew that solar power had a bad rap and was perceived as overly expensive. For people to choose solar, we had to find a way to get the audience to see just how much money a solar panel system would save them each and every month. We had to position it not as a cost, but as an investment that would pay off.

Instead of writing an article on savings, we decided to create a custom *solar design tool* that allowed potential customers to enter their address, view actual satellite imagery of their house, and then design/layout a solar panel system in a Google Maps style view of their property (see Figure 6.1).

FIGURE 6.1   **Put solar panels on a satellite image of your roof and see what you can save.**

Once they've added solar panels to the real photo of their roof, they can see how much they can expect to save with the system they designed. It's a simple and engaging tool that solves the users' problem in an interesting way.

Once they see that they're saving a few hundred dollars a month on their energy bill, they're much more likely to submit their information to request a formal quote.

Another great example is a campaign that a friend and fellow digital creative director named Todd Slutzky worked on while he was at VML.

The challenge they were given was to convince moms to prepare for flu season by purchasing Kleenex. Instead of advertising tissues in a traditional manner, or creating blog posts and articles reminding people that flu season was around the corner, they decided to design and build an interactive flu prediction tool that helped moms find out when they were most at risk for the flu in their area (see Figure 6.2).

The result of this clever idea was coverage in *Fast Company*, *Ad Age*, and numerous other publications. It also brought home a Webby for it's innovative approach to solving the problem.

Even if the content you'd like to create isn't budgeted for as part of the original scope of work, if your idea is a good one and you state your case well, then it's likely the client will give you additional budget to make it happen.

Clients want to be innovative as much as you do. Never be afraid to present a good idea for making content more interactive and compelling. The worst thing that can happen is they say no.

**FIGURE 6.2    Kleenex's flu prediction tool.**

## Simple Content Well-Executed Can Be Really Effective

Even if you can't find ways to push content into interactive forms, if the content you create is valuable and informative, then it will still have value.

The opposite is true as well. All the bells and whistles in the world won't matter if the content doesn't connect with the audience.

## Entertaining a Cynical Audience

Back when films were first invented you could pack a theater with a novelty video of a train arriving at a station. That's no longer the case. Our standards for entertainment are higher now. Everyone in our modern society is now an expert consumer of entertainment.

We also have much more refined B.S. detectors. We're a cynical bunch—ready to roll our eyes at the scent of anything that seems overly sales-y or self-promotional.

This means our expectations for the types of content that brands produce is higher.

But it's not hopeless. Humans are story-telling animals and crave entertainment. Long before the written word our species was sitting around fires telling tales about wise chiefs, great hunts, and doomed love.

If you want to create entertainment, you have to tell an interesting story.

## What If I Don't Have an Interesting Story to Tell?

Some of you may be saying to yourself that there are no stories worth telling about your client or your brand, but that's a cop out.

FIGURE 6.3    **Coke manufactures myth. Not soft drinks. (Reprinted from Getty Images, Seattle, WA. With permission.)**

Take Coke for example. Coke doesn't manufacture soft drinks. It manufactures myth. It manufactures stories. If it can tell a story about fizzy sugar water, then you can tell a story about anything (see Figure 6.3).

## Create Something That's Interesting to the Audience

The biggest mistake we make as creators of content is that we assume the audience cares about the same things we do. This is rarely true.

We have to be brutally honest and say: would the audience care about this? If so, why? Will it make them think, laugh, or smile? If not, go back to the drawing board and find something that touches them and provokes a reaction.

## All Great Stories Revolve Around Conflict and Tension

At the heart of any compelling story is some sort of conflict. Conflict creates interest. Without some sort of conflict, there is no point to the story. There's no tension, there's no good guy, and no bad guy. Without conflict, nothing happens.

There are numerous ways you can bring tension and conflict into the content you craft. It could be conflict between your brand and another brand, conflict between the way things are versus the way things should be, conflict between opposing ideologies, conflict between your current self and your better self, or conflict between a hero and a villain.

It often helps to exaggerate these tensions or conflicts to drive your ideas. The world is rarely black and white, but nuanced stories are tough to tell in the limited format of the digital world. Your goal is to amplify tension, not reduce it.

## The Reason Theme Parks Have Castles and What You Can Learn From It

Walt Disney was of the firm belief that every theme park needed a dramatic element that was large enough to be noticed from anywhere, and interesting enough to draw people toward it to take a closer look. It would also be the thing you remembered about visiting the park. He called these design elements *Weenies* (Fischer 2004).

You can apply this same thinking to the digital experiences you build. Each website should have a piece of tent pole content that acts like a castle in a theme park. It should be memorable and remarkable. It could be a fantastic video, beautiful data visualization, a really useful tool, or an engaging interactive experience.

These types of content experiences are the difference between a good website and a great one.

## Advice on Producing Videos and Animation

As the web has grown more interactive, video is playing a larger role in the digital experience. As a modern digital creative director, you'll need to be comfortable producing video for the web.

There are a million different ways to categorize video projects, but a few of the most common are as follows:

## Motion Graphics and Animation Videos

These pieces rely mainly on animation to communicate their message. Think kinetic type, infographic-style visuals, and simple character animations set to music and voiceover.

They're great for telling simple stories, introducing abstract concepts, and highlighting interesting facts. You'll want to keep them short and sweet, as the style grows tiresome after a minute or two. We'll often recommend the motion graphics/animation approach when budgets are tight, and there's not a physical product to highlight.

Unless you know Adobe After Effects or another animation platform, you'll want to work with a motion graphics studio/freelancer on production. You'll need to decide whether or not you will create the storyboards that show what each frame of the animation is, or whether they will.

Always make sure to get your storyboards approved by client before entering production. Making changes in the preanimation phase will always be cheaper. If you're doing pencil/pen storyboards, then it's also helpful to create some full color-style boards to help show what the end product will look like.

Licensing music is easier than it's ever been. Sites like pumpaudio.com and marmosetmusic.com make it easy to search for music to license. Oftentimes this is the easiest route, but it's not your only option.

You can also look to local artists and producers to see if they would be willing to produce a custom score. The price is often inexpensive and the advantage of a custom score is that it can easily be modified to match the specific emotional tone of the end product.

Voiceover work is also really easy to source via the web. Sites like voice123. com let you search for talent and request auditions from specific artists, or simply post your project and allow anyone to audition.

## Film- and Commercial-Style Videos

A film- and commercial-style production is very structured. These types of productions require a strong script, good actors, and professional production to be successful.

Generally, they're more expensive than purely animated pieces due to the complexity of production.

Everything is planned to the smallest detail and if anything goes off track, your costs can rise pretty dramatically. If you don't have experience producing or managing a shoot, it's helpful to bring in a director to help set budget early in the process.

A good director will give you feedback on the script, scout locations/talent, create detailed shot lists, and help manage every aspect of the production to ensure a great result. These shoots are very much a one and done opportunity, so make sure you get everything you need during the shoot.

You'll want to be on-site during the production, but be sure that your role is clearly defined prior to the shoot and you're not stepping on the director's toes by trying to backseat drive the production.

A good director will also help manage postproduction (color, motion, etc.) and editing.

Once the edited piece is completed, be sure to give detailed feedback. Including the time stamp at which something occurs will make their job much easier. Don't necessarily try to solve every issue. Instead, bring up the problem and ask for suggestions to solve it.

## Documentary-Style Videos

A documentary-style production is a slightly different animal. These are usually interview-heavy. You'll still do a lot of planning, scouting, and pre-production work, but you won't really know what you have until the shoot is complete and you get in the editing room.

With this type of production, identifying interesting subjects and developing great interview questions is key. No amount of beautiful b-roll footage will save the video if the content isn't strong. A director with strong editing skills and lots of experience with these types of productions will make your life much easier.

These types of productions work great when the story you want to tell can be told from multiple points of view. They tend to feel more authentic and believable. But they're also risky in that you may find yourself without a coherent story at the end and need additional footage to tie it altogether.

## Designing Infographics in the Age of Big Data

Back in 1983 when Edward R. Tufte published his book, *The Visual Display of Quantitative Data*, infographics were largely the trade of education and news publications. Information design was generally thought of in terms of simple pie charts and bar graphs.

But with the rise of the Internet, the popularity of the infographic as a form of visual communication skyrocketed.

They're an ideal form of visual communication for the web. They're easy to create, easy to read, and easy to share. As a result, brands have realized that they're a great way to get attention from content-hungry web publishers.

So how do you actually go about designing an infographic that resonates?

### Do Your Homework and Compile Your Research

At the heart of information design is information. You have to start by gathering all the relevant data you can find about a topic. Don't just scan it. Try to understand the relationship between the data points and the context around it.

### Weave Facts Together in a Broader Narrative That Makes a Statement

Once you have the facts, it's time to craft a narrative and a story around them. The goal is to find a story that's worth telling—something that will interest and intrigue your audience. Ideally the story that emerges combines all the separate facts into a cohesive narrative.

### Use Visual Metaphors and Sketch the Most Interesting Facts

There are endless ways to represent data. Start with the most impactful data point you have and begin exploring ways to represent it in a compelling manner. As you think through visual forms, try to identify ways that you can use design as a shortcut to communicate more information more quickly, and brainstorm visual metaphors that could be illustrated around the topic.

## If You're Not a Strong Illustrator, Hire One

Information design can be done well with simple graphics and typography. But the best infographics usually have a component of custom illustration. If you're not strong in this skillset, look to hire someone who is. If you've done the hard work of gathering the data, weaving the narrative and having an idea for visual metaphors, then they'll be able to quickly create a beautiful illustration.

## Finding and Working with Production Partners

No one is great at everything, so being able to find top-notch production partners that can fill the gaps in your expertise is a vital skill.

### Nothing Beats Recommendations from Friends and Colleagues

Start by asking friends and colleagues if they have any recommendations. But make sure you're specific about the project. For example, say *I'm looking for a architectural photographer with experience shooting restaurants in Atlanta* versus *I'm looking for a photographer.*

### Fish Where the Fish Live

You'll also want to start looking on the web. Specific Google searches are great, but you can also search industry-specific social networks. If you're looking for an illustrator, search dribble.com. If you're looking for a videographer, search vimeo.com. If you're looking for infographic illustrators, search visual.ly.

   As you search and review their work, also make note of any reference pieces that you like. They may be in a cool style, or solve similar challenges.

### Quality of Work Is More Important Than Industry and Brand Experience

When looking for a partner, the most important thing is the quality of work they've produced. It's great if they have experience working in the industry of the client, but it shouldn't be a requirement.

As you're reviewing the work, try to get insight into the role they played in the project. Someone may be a great animator, but his or her best work might have been storyboarded by an outside art director. Ask about the details of the project to ensure the work they've shown accurately represents their capabilities.

## Share Scope and Budget at the Beginning of the Conversation

Once you've found a partner you want to work with, start the conversation around scope, availability, and budget right away. If they're not available, or budgets aren't aligned, you don't want to waste anyone's time.

Give a broad overview of the general idea, the goal of the end product and any specific details around your expectations for them as far as their role in the project. To help communicate scope, it's often helpful to include reference pieces similar in style and production to what you're envisioning. You'll also want to make sure that your project manager is kept in the loop throughout these conversations.

After that, it's as simple as getting a formal estimate/proposal and starting work.

## The Siren Song of Mediocrity Will Try to Tempt You

Sure it's easier to just warm over existing content and spiffy it up with a fresh new design, but that's a road that leads straight to mediocrity.

If you want to create work that moves the needle, the content your site contains deserves as much attention as the design it's wrapped in. I hope you'll give it the attention it deserves.

## References

Fischer, R. January 01, 2004. The creation of Disneyland. http://www.plosin.com/beatbegins/projects/fischer.html. Accessed on January 15, 2015.

Leslie, E. 2015. *The Story of Content: Rise of the New Marketing*. Director-Eric Leslie, Kinonation, Streaming.

Tufte, E. R. 1983. *The Visual Display of Quantitative Information*. Graphics Press, Cheshire, CT.

Zeldman, J. 2009. A Design Apart Q&A – Zeldman on Web interaction. http://www.zeldman.com/2009/11/19/a-design-apart-qa/. Accessed on April 18, 2016.

# Chapter 7

# Making Your Message Spread

*The secret to success? Be so good they can't ignore you.*

***Steve Martin***

The most valuable currencies in the modern world are ideas and attention. As a creative director, your goal isn't just to design a website or an app. It's to get your idea to spread, and win the war for attention.

This is a difficult task, mainly because people have been trained to ignore you. In order to survive the onslaught of advertising and marketing that we're exposed to on a daily basis, we've become really good at ignoring messages.

Out of the thousands of marketing messages that you're exposed to each day, how many do you remember? How many made you take an action? How many did you share? The answer is likely well below 0.1%.

That's what we're going to tackle in this chapter. We'll attempt to answer the question of how do you make your message spread in today's hypercompetitive media environment?

We'll discuss why some content is shared more than others, how to engineer virality into a campaign, and how doing stuff worth talking about is the secret to getting people to pay attention.

# What Types of Content Are Most Likely to Be Shared and Why?

Why are some types of content shared more often than others? In 2009, Jonah Berger and Katherine Milkman tried to solve this riddle. They studied how often people shared *New York Times* articles published over a three-month period, the types of content those articles contained, and the emotions those articles evoked (Milkman 2009).

The results of this study are worth talking about in more detail.

## Content That Inspires High-Energy Emotions Like Awe, Anxiety, or Anger Is Shared More Than Content That Inspires Low-Energy Emotions Like Sadness

It's common sense to think that content that is emotionally impactful is more likely to be shared, but one of the more interesting findings is that the type of emotion that the content inspires has an effect on the likelihood that it will be shared.

Articles that inspired anger and allowed the audience to connect with their frustrations around a topic were more likely to be shared than any other type. Closely followed by those that inspired awe (e.g., a new discovery or an inspiration story of overcoming adversity) and anxiety (e.g., reports of negative economic news). These types of emotions inspire what psychologists refer to as heightened activation and this leads to a higher propensity toward sharing.

This is the secret behind the rapid growth of companies like Upworthy, which *Fast Company* called the fastest growing media site of all time (Kamenetz 2013). Their whole business model is based on finding content that evokes strong high-energy emotions and optimizing its virality through clickbait headlines, imagery, and UX.

Take heed, if you want your message to spread, it has to evoke a strong emotional response.

## Long Form Content Is More Likely to Be Shared than Short-Form Content

It's said that people on the Internet have limited attention spans, but that doesn't mean they won't consume longer form content. In fact, engaging with content at a deeper level makes it more likely to be shared. In Berger and Milkman's research (2009), they found that the length of an article had the strongest correlation to whether or not it was likely to be shared.

Even after they controlled for factors like the amount of exposure it was given on the homepage.

And this doesn't just hold for articles. It applies to content of all types. When the TED organization first started putting their conference videos online in 2006, people were of the belief that the Internet would only share short humorous videos. They scoffed at the idea that people would watch an 18-minute talk online.

Not only did they watch them, they shared them at astounding rate. By 2012, TED talks had been viewed more than one billion times (Sapling Foundation 2012).

The lesson is simple: don't be afraid of long form high-quality content. It's more likely to be shared than any other type.

## Content That Has Practical Utility Is Most Likely to Be Shared

Another finding from their research is that useful, practical content was shared at a higher rate than other content.

Useful content taps into two types of motivations: altruism and self-enhancement. People share it because they want to help others (e.g., voter guides for an upcoming election), or they share it because they want to appear knowledgeable and informed to their friends (e.g., a TED talk on the power of body language).

So don't be afraid to craft content that takes advantage of this fact. Really useful content will always find an audience.

## Humor Is Powerful

While Berger and Milkman's study (2009) brings forth some interesting facts, it does have one major limitation. Since it relied on the *New York Times* as its source for data, not all content types are well-represented. For instance, there aren't many funny or humorous articles in the *New York Times.* So is the idea of a funny viral video a myth? Nope. Humor might just be the most powerful emotion of all.

A study by Rosanna E. Guadagno of the National Science Foundation actually found that funny/cute videos were more likely to be shared than videos that provoked anger/disgust (Jaffe 2014).

So don't overlook humor as a way to make your content more share-worthy.

Now that we've talked about the types of content that are likely to get shared and why people share it, let's discuss a term that every creative director I know loathes: *viral.*

# What People Get Wrong About Viral Campaigns?

When marketers talk about something going viral, they're generally referring to a viral meme. These are pieces of content that just happen to hit a nerve in popular culture and spread at an astronomical rate. You can think of them like shooting stars. They spread fast and then they disappear.

One day someone uploads a video of a dog in a spider costume on YouTube, and 12 months later it's been viewed 127 million times.

Too often marketers strive to replicate this success. The warning signs are clear. They'll say they want to do something viral and mention whatever happens to be popular in the cultural zeitgeist at that moment.

These campaigns almost always fail. They fail because memes are unpredictable. They require an adoption by the greater culture that is completely random. This doesn't mean you shouldn't create fun and entertaining content. You should, but don't create it because you expect it to go viral. The chances are it never will.

However, there is a second type of virality that can be engineered. In fact, the most successful campaigns make it a key element of their approach.

## Building Virality into Your Campaigns

In 2014, a viral fundraising campaign called the Ice Bucket Challenge took the social media by storm. In less than a month it had raised more than $50 million dollars for the ALS charities (*TIME* 2014).

The reason this campaign was so successful had little to do with the ice bucket or the worthiness of the cause. They didn't run TV commercials or cover the web in banner ads promoting the cause. The reason it was successful was the fact that it was engineered for virality.

There are a couple of key factors that led to its phenomenal rise.

## Why the Ice Bucket Challenge Worked

The basis of the campaign was viral in nature. People issued a challenge to their friends: you could either donate $100 to an ALS charity, or douse yourself with ice, film it, and pass the challenge on to others via social media.

Each person who was challenged in turn challenged others. Sharing was a part of the campaign itself. On account of this, it spread like wildfire.

## It Was Highly Visible and Allowed People to Present Themselves as Charitable to the Wider World

It's no secret that most things shared on social media shed a positive light on the sharer. Since this was a charitable cause, the Ice Bucket Challenge was an easy way to show your friends, family, and acquaintances that you cared about charity. Even better, there was a video recording of you participating in it. It was the perfect way to seek attention in a way that could still seem humble. It also created a shareable asset to help promote the campaign.

And since you were challenged publicly, there was really no easy way to decline the challenge without seeming uncharitable. Therefore, there was social pressure to participate.

## Celebrity Participation Helped Spark the Flame

The challenge really started to gain steam when a professional Supercross rider Jeremy McGrath called out a professional golfer named Keegan Bradley to participate in the challenge.

From there it spread throughout the pro golf circuit to media celebrities such as Matt Lauer and Martha Stewart, and numerous others. This gave it greater exposure in popular culture and a sense of legitimacy that it might not have had otherwise. Soon media publications across the United States were writing and filming news stories on the challenge, spurring a media and organizational arms race of participation, further fueling it's rapid growth.

It was a campaign that was built to spread and it did, raising unprecedented levels of awareness for ALS and driving more than $50 million dollars in donations in the process.

## Want People to Pay Attention?
## Do Stuff Worth Talking About

Too much of marketing and advertising is about spreading a message, and while that worked throughout most of the twentieth century, it's no longer enough. You can't just design a new website or campaign and say, *My job is done. Now it's up to the media planner.*

If you want to break through the clutter of the thousands of messages we're blasted with each and every day you have to take a different approach. You have to do stuff worth talking about.

So how do you go about doing things worth talking about?

Think to yourself, if I were a member of the target audience would I share it with my friends? Does it give me a story that helps me tell the world the type of person I am? Is it something I would watch, video, or photograph if I was there?

## Don't Limit Yourself to Things That Happen Only in the Digital Space

Often real-life events are more interesting and compelling than things that only take place in the digital space. But they drive huge interest and activity online. As a digital creative director, you're making a mistake if you limit yourself to things that happen only online.

For example, in 2013 we decided to promote a campaign called #ChooseATL at the SXSW Interactive festival in Austin, TX. The goal was to create an online buzz at the world's largest interactive festival.

Instead of buying banner ads on SXSW's site or sponsoring event e-mails, we decided to do something completely different. We threw a spontaneous, flash-mob-style lantern parade and marched down the heart of SXSW interactive.

Lantern parades are actually an Atlanta tradition where 20,000 plus people take to the Atlanta BeltLine with homemade lanterns and light up the sky in a show of city pride and creativity. We wanted to bring this slice of culture to SXSW.

In order to pull this off, we hired a small marching band, built a list of Atlantans that were attending the conference so we could recruit them to march in the parade, held lantern-building parties prior to the conference and built giant walking puppets (see Figure 7.1).

This offline activity drew online attention. During the night of the parade, our hashtag trended on twitter thanks to the hundreds of folks who ran out

FIGURE 7.1    Putting on a parade for #ChooseATL at the SXSW Interactive festival (Austin, TX).

of the bars on Sixth Street in Austin, grabbed their camera, and took photos capturing the event.

It cost us about $5,000 to pull it off and we got more attention than brands that spent 10 times as much money on conventional activities.

## If It's Not Difficult to Pull Off, Then It's Probably Not Worth Doing

Red Bull understands this better than almost any brand out there. The Red Bull Stratos campaign was a great example of a real-life activity that drove enormous online results (see Figure 7.2).

The initial idea was ambitious and remarkable. Let's send a man into the stratosphere and have him parachute back down to Earth in order to break the world record for highest altitude skydive. It was a way to bring the Red Bull brand to life by pushing the limits of human achievement.

But it wasn't easy. It took seven years of planning to make it happen. I was stressed out planning a parade. I can't imagine what the folks at Red Bull felt when they were trying to send a guy into space and record the entirety of the jump live from multiple angles.

But because of its audacity and the difficulty in pulling it off, the results were as remarkable as the event itself.

More than eight million people watched the jump live on YouTube (a new record) and the free media exposure generated by the stunt was worth tens of millions of dollars (WPP Inc. 2013).

The lesson is simple. If you want your message to spread, the best thing to do is make it worth talking about.

FIGURE 7.2    **Red Bull pushed the limits of human achievement and captured our attention. (Reprinted from Red Bull Media House, Salzburg, Austria. With permission.)**

# References

Jaffe, E. February 17, 2014. These scientists studied why internet stories go viral. You won't believe what they found. *Fast Company*. http://www.fastcodesign.com/3024276/evidence/these-scientists-studied-why-internet-stories-go-viral-you-wont-believe-what-they-f. Accessed on January 16, 2015.

Kamenetz, A. June 07, 2013. How Upworthy used emotional data to become the fastest growing media site of all time. *Fast Company*. http://www.fastcompany.com/3012649/how-upworthy-used-emotional-data-to-become-the-fastest-growing-media-site-of-all-time. Accessed on January 15, 2015.

Milkman, K. L. and Berger, J. A. December 25, 2009. What makes online content viral. *Social Science Research Network*. http://papers.ssrn.com/sol3/papers.cfm?abstract_id=1528077. Accessed on January 28, 2015.

Sapling Foundation. November 13, 2012. TED reaches its billionth video view! http://blog.ted.com/2012/11/13/ted-reaches-its-billionth-video-view/. Accessed on January 16, 2015.

*TIME*. August 22, 2014. Ice bucket challenge ALS donations break $50 million mark. *TIME*. http://time.com/3159673/als-ice-bucket-challenge-donations/. Accessed on April 18, 2016.

WPP Inc. March 07, 2013. Red Bull Stratos. *WPP Reading Room*. http://www.wpp.com/wpp/marketing/digital/red-bull-stratos/. Accessed on January 16, 2015.

# Section II

## Building and Showing

# Chapter 8

# The Digital Design Process

*I have not failed. I've just found 10,000 ways that won't work.*

*Thomas Edison*

We've talked a lot about understanding users, brand, and digital strategy. Now it's time to dive deep into the digital design process.

As a digital creative director, it's your job to manage this process from start to finish. That's what this chapter is about. We'll also talk about how this process changes depending on whether you're working in an agile or waterfall environment.

Before we dive into the process discussion, I want to clear up a misconception that sometimes exists. It's the idea that user experience doesn't fall into the realm of creative direction. This is simply not true. If you're going to be held accountable for delighting the target audience, then user experience is one of the most important aspects of your job.

## The Key Steps in the Digital Experience Design Process

1. *Define content and functionality*: This is where the process starts. Some people might call it *information architecture*. Others may refer to it as *experience mapping*. No matter what it's called, the goal of this phase

is to define the user's journey, the devices, touch points and content they'll interact with, and the functional requirements around each step in the journey.

2. *Design the overarching layout and form*: Out of all the phases, this is the one that usually gets the most attention and it's also considered the most fun. It's where visual interface designs, navigation schemes, and initial design patterns are developed for the overarching experience. The design concepts in this phase set the stage for the rest of the process.

3. *Prototype the experience and craft interactions*: Once we've defined the overarching user interface concept, then we can move into creating detailed wireframes and high-fidelity prototypes for the rest of the experience. The goal of this phase is to think through the various detailed interface states and interactions. From simple interactions, like the hover state for a button, to detailed prototypes of complex experiences that contain multiple steps. The reason we prototype is that it enables us to easily gather feedback, test our design decisions, and iterate quickly.

4. *Create detailed designs*: After we've prototyped the experience, then we can start working on the detailed designs for each of the states and interactions for each of the stages of the user's journey. The result of this stage is that every aspect of the interface is now designed with intention and a strong aesthetic point of view.

5. *Review the final product and make it better*: After detailed designs are implemented, it's time to review the product to identify potential issues and opportunities for improvement. In this phase, we want to strive for a level of polish and perfection that will result in user delight.

6. *Test your assumptions*: The last phase is perhaps the most important. It's where we get to test our assumptions and see how our work resonates with real users.

## Defining Content and Functionality Across Screens and Platforms

Experience mapping is the art of organizing a site's content and structure in an intuitive manner. The outcome of this process is a flow chart, site map, or outline of the key screens or pages that the user will encounter along with a rationale that explains the goals and intended outcomes of each screen.

When the web was a medium mostly accessed through the traditional desktops, this process was pretty simple. Back in the early days of the Internet, most people only had a single computer with a single screen. The single screen was the only thing you had to design for.

Today, screens are everywhere and they run a wide variety of platforms and operating systems. There are screens for reading, for watching, for interacting, for working, and for playing. The nature of our interaction with those screens has changed pretty dramatically as well. Screens were once only used for output. Now gesture and touch is everywhere.

This means we're now designing systems that have to work across platforms and devices.

It's up to you to figure out what devices and touch points need to be designed and how they'll interact together.

If the project is a website for a corporate client, then it could be as simple as a responsive design that shows the same content to users regardless of the device they're using. The only difference across screens and platforms is that you'll have to design for multiple screen sizes.

If it's something more complex, let's say the redesign of the entire digital experience for a major transit system, then it could include a whole ecosystem of devices and platforms (see Figure 8.1).

## Map Out the Devices and Platforms You'll Need to Design For and How They Interact with One Another

Start by asking which platform/screen (web, app, or other) will be the most highly utilized. Now that you've figured out which one is the *home base* then start thinking through how the other interfaces will interact with them.

Will the interface have the same general experience across all devices, and exist independent of one another? This is the approach of most responsive websites. What happens on one device isn't reflected on any other device.

FIGURE 8.1   A complex experience map can span devices and platforms.

Or will the devices work as a single ecosystem with all actions automatically synchronizing across all the other devices? This approach is common with connected devices like the Nest thermostat.

If you change to the temperature of the thermostat, that change is reflected on the Nest website, and native apps automatically. They work together seamlessly as a unit. It's an ecosystem that works across multiple screens and platforms.

## Think in Terms of Flow, Not Pages

There's a tendency when starting this process to focus on the individual screens/pages that the user will interact with, what they're named, and the order they're arranged in.

But how the pages are arranged (or even what they're named) is less important than whether or not there is an intuitive path for the user to follow that will help them reach their goal.

When looking at experience maps, put yourself in the user's shoes and see if you'd be able to navigate the journey across the different device types and touch points they'll interact with. Make sure that each screen or page that the user interacts with clearly directs them to the next step they'll need to take to accomplish their goal.

A helpful metaphor is that of a scent trail. Users are constantly looking for contextual clues that help them find what they're seeking. If the scent is strong, then they can easily follow the path and reach their goals, but if the scent dies any point during their journey, then they end up lost, and the digital experience fails.

## Always Strive to Simplify Complex Navigation

When you're designing a content-heavy site (like an ecommerce store for instance), it's really easy to make a site's navigation scheme overly complex—a nest of categories, subcategories, and sub-sub categories that may have a clear sense of hierarchy, but will be a nightmare for a user to navigate.

Try to keep navigation to as few levels as possible. Fewer levels mean fewer clicks for the user to get where they want to go, and less complexity to design for.

As you look at a site's content, try to find opportunities to streamline. Seek out potentially redundant content, and try to reorganize it in a more simplified manner. Remember that key content can easily be linked across pages and sections so there's no need for the same content to live in multiple places.

## Conventional Navigation Names and Labels Aren't Something to Be Avoided

During this process, there is often a temptation to try and come up with a cooler way to say something. At some point you will hear something like, *Everyone says "shop" on their website we should call it something cooler.* And while all want to be unique and interesting, it's often best avoided.

Plain language navigation and labels generally work because users understand them. Try to avoid jargon, don't use slogans as navigation items and don't try to be overly cute. Navigation and labels are a tool, not a branding opportunity.

## Architect for Future Change

Stewart Brand (1994) once said, "All buildings are predictions. All predictions are wrong." This is also true for experience mapping. Good experience design should be flexible and scalable enough to meet the future business needs of the client.

## Make Sure There Are Opportunities for Delight

One of the reasons it's important you participate in this process is that you want to make sure that there is an opportunity to create something remarkable.

Look for opportunities to create moments of delight. This is your chance to share all those cool content ideas you came up with in Chapter 6, even if you're not 100% sure on the execution. If it's not in the experience map, it won't be in the final product.

## How to Evaluate and Critique Experience Maps?

To help evaluate the proposed content and functionality for a project, ask yourself the following questions.

- Does the breakdown of device and the way those devices interact make sense?
- Is there a clear path for users to follow that will allow them to reach their goals?
- Does the content meet the needs of the user during each phase of the buyer journey? Are there any key pieces that are missing?
- Does the taxonomy/classification scheme of content make sense to an end user?

- Are things named and labeled in a way that a user will understand them?
- Is it flexible enough to meet the future business needs of the client?
- Is there an opportunity to do something that creates a moment of delight?

## Designing the Overarching Layout and Form

Now that we've nailed down the devices we're designing for along with the content and its functionality, it's time to get your design team working on layout concepts. We talked a lot about elements of great design in Chapter 4, so in this chapter we're going to focus more on the details of the design process.

### Deciding Who Works on the Design

Depending on the size of your design team and the current workload, you may be able to assign multiple designers to the project. If so, that's great. However, just because a project calls for designing multiple initial concepts, don't feel like you have to assign a unique designer for each one.

I've found that it's often better to have a single designer spend more time working on multiple concepts for a single project, rather than splitting the concepts between multiple designers. That's because a single designer is forced to go deeper in the design process if they're responsible for multiple directions. It also reduces the amount of communication required throughout the design process. You can give feedback once instead of twice.

If two designers are assigned to a project, you'll often find their initial directions are really similar. Since the most straightforward design solution is the easiest one to come up with, you'll often see that both designers arrived at very similar solutions. You can avoid this issue if you take the paper-before-pixels approach that we discuss a later in this chapter.

### How to Pick What Part of the Project to Design First?

Designing a big interactive project is like eating an elephant. The only way to succeed is bite by bite.

Start by trying to solve the most difficult design challenge on the most important device type first. By tackling the most complex interface first, you can ensure that the most challenging part of the project gets allocated the most amount of time for research, thinking, and iteration.

If you're designing a marketing website, this will probably be the homepage, but if you're designing an app, it's probably a dashboard, or it could be the control screen of a connected device.

## Briefing Your Design Team on the Project

Now that we know what we're asking the team to design and who is going to work on it, it's time to schedule a design briefing.

At this point in the project you should have a project/creative brief, user personas, an experience map, and any brand guidelines and creative assets from the client. Package these items up and deliver them to your design team so they can review before you schedule a briefing.

At the actual briefing, you'll want to review a few key things:

- *The design goal*: What is the single most important thing this design needs to accomplish?
- *Touch points and device types*: Review the experience map and the different touch points across devices. It's important to mention any constraints that the design team needs to be aware of for each device type.
- *The competitive space*: Who are the main competitors? What makes this client different? Is there anything noteworthy about the category?
- *The target audience personas*: Who is the target audience? What are they trying to accomplish? How do they perceive the brand/market?
- *Creative thought starters*: Talk through any key insights you have. Are there cultural tensions that should be explored? What is the most honest and true thing you can say about the brand? Are there reference sites that have tackled similar challenges that are worth reviewing? Are there sites that the client liked/disliked that you can point to?
- *Success measurements*: Include how you'll actually be measuring success. You've already outlined the goal, but what key performance indicators will you use to show you succeeded?
- *Deliverables expected and timelines*: Make sure your designers have a strong understanding of the deliverables you're expecting and by when. It's wise to schedule work in progress reviews at this point as well. Schedule reviews for sketches, early drafts, and final work.

It's easy to assume that the designers have read the documents, and that they automatically know as much about the project as you do. But it's often a mistake to do so. By holding more structured design briefings, you can ensure that all that important knowledge is transferred to the team executing your vision and it will help the process go more smoothly.

## Paper Before Pixels

Your design team will probably want to start by opening Photoshop and getting right to work. But first have them pull out the pencil and paper to sketch their initial concepts. The reason they should start with sketches is that it's an easy way to visualize and iterate a large variety of layouts quickly.

Have the designer(s) working on the project develop at least 10 unique interface sketches that show different ways you could showcase content and handle navigation.

The sketches don't have to be large. A quarter page is more than enough room to capture the initial idea. Encourage them to look at design awards sites for ideas and inspiration. Have them try to adapt approaches they like to the design challenge you're trying to solve.

As they work through sketches, encourage them to aim for variation. Try placing navigation in different areas of the page. Play around with icon-based versus text-based navigation labels. Think through ways that navigation could shift as the user interacts with the page to get out of the way of the content. Explore different styles and treatments for copy and image areas. The goal at this point is iteration and volume.

Once the team has completed sketches, select a few of the strongest sketch concepts and have each designer create high-fidelity presentation-ready design comps based on the concept they sketched.

## How to Evaluate and Critique Design?

One of the most important aspects of your job is going to be reviewing and critiquing design work, not only from a visual standpoint, but also from a conceptual standpoint.

## Visual Elements to Evaluate during a Design Review

Start by looking at the core visual elements. These 10 elements aren't absolute, but they provide a good framework for feedback.

As you review the design, think about each of the elements below.

- *Hierarchy*: Does the layout reflect the relative importance of each item it contains? Is there a structure and pattern that's pleasing to the eye? Is there a clear single area of focus?
- *Contrast*: Is there enough contrast between elements? Are important elements highlighted in a way that provides emphasis?
- *Balance*: Does the design feel well-balanced? Does the sum of each element add to it's greater whole?

- *Areas of focus*: Does the design have a sense of depth? Even *flat design* when done well establishes a foreground and background to create a clear areas of focus.
- *Cohesiveness*: Does the design feel cohesive and consistent in its use of visual elements? Is there a coherent use of design elements (texture, type, color)?
- *Color*: How well are the colors within the design working together? Is the color palette appropriate and well thought out?
- *Ease of use*: How easy to use is the interface itself? Are difficult tasks broken into smaller, easier steps? Are there clear and easy to understand paths for users to follow so they can accomplish their goals (calls-to-action, etc.)?
- *Typography*: Does the design make strong use of typography? Does the typeface reflect the voice of the brand/message? Is the typeface for body copy easy to read? Is the leading and sentence length appropriate?
- *Personality*: Does the design reflect the personality of the brand? Does it have a clear point of view and set of beliefs?
- *Adaptability*: How will the design work across various device types? Will it be easy to use on mobile and tablet? Are there elements that will need to change to make it more responsive?

## Questions to Ask When Evaluating Design

To help evaluate the design based on nonaesthetic attributes, answer the following questions.

- *How does this design support the overall objective/goals?* Not only the business goals, but also the goals of the user.
- *Is it emotionally impactful?* Design should emotionally engage an audience. Does it resonate emotionally, or make me laugh/smile/ think? What type of person would love this? Who would hate it?
- *Does this embody the brand?* Is the work aligned with the brand personality and tone that you're trying to convey?
- *Would the media care about this?* If so, what would the headline be? Great ideas spread via earned media and word of mouth. If there's no clear reason for people to care, then it's likely to be ignored.
- *Is it innovative in it's use of content or interactivity?* Does the experience bring something new to the table? It could be a unique piece of content that your target audience will find valuable, or an interactive tool that helps them in an engaging way.
- *Are we thinking big enough?* Is it ambitious enough in scope and execution to be considered remarkable?

- *What would make someone want to share this?* Why would someone send this to another person? Is there a way to engineer virality and encourage people to share it?
- *How can it be better?* This is the most important question. Look for rough spots that could use polish and areas that could be improved. The goal is to make every detail as perfect as possible.

## Prototyping the Experience and Crafting Interactions

Now that we have the layout and form designed, it's time to prototype out the rest of the experience.

Wireframe prototypes can take many forms, and they can be created using a wide variety of tools. In an ideal scenario, the prototype will be built in as close to the final form as possible. This means that if it's a website, the interactive wireframes should be made in HTML. If it's an app, then they should be built in the preferred language of that platform (e.g., Objective C, Embedded C, Java, or Swift).

There are a few key advantages to taking this approach. The first big advantage is that it's more representative of what the end product will be, and because it's built in the same form as the final product, it's not a dead-end deliverable that just gets created once and then thrown away never to be used again. Once your prototype is created, it can actually serve as the basis for your development efforts later in the project. This makes the overall build process more efficient.

The second big advantage is that you can test the experience natively on the device so you can identify and settle any big issues early. If something is difficult to do at this early stage, then you still have plenty of time to find alternative solutions. By understanding constraints earlier in the process, you can avoid compromises later. This is especially important when using platforms that you're not as familiar with.

Now you may argue that it's unrealistic to take this approach. That it requires a developer and that it will take too much time. But I've found this approach actually helps make projects flow smoother and go faster. If you can, do it.

## Don't Prototype Templates, Prototype the User's Journey

Instead of just listing out a series of templates, try to prototype a user's journey from start to finish.

By taking a scenario-based approach, you can prioritize the elements of the user experience that are most important to the target audience. This allows you to test a realistic version of the experience from start to finish.

## Collaboration Is Key

At this point in the process, I've found it works best to take a highly collaborative approach. Have the design and the front-end development teams work together closely.

There's no need to go back into Photoshop or other design tools. Have the team sketch out the rest of the interface screens based on the patterns and approach defined in the approved visual design concept.

From there, the development team can use those sketches to build out the remainder of the prototype directly in code. It's ok if your prototype is a little rough at this phase. A prototype isn't supposed to be perfectly polished.

## Focus on Creating Reusable Design Patterns

Throughout this process, try to limit the visual complexity of your interfaces so that it behaves consistently from one screen to the next.

Things like consistent use of a grid, typographic styles, interaction patterns and button styles, and consistent system-level interactions are all things you want to keep an eye out for.

## Avoid Using *lorem ipsum* Whenever Possible

As you go through this process, there will be a temptation to use *lorem ipsum* text to fill in the gaps in content. The argument for *lorem ipsum* is that Greek text is a great placeholder for content and it's easy.

While it's true that it's easy—it takes what should be a high-fidelity concept, and makes it low fidelity. Instead of a prototype, you end up with a bunch of grey boxes and Greek text. You can't separate content from design.

That's why you should try to use realistic placeholder copy. A rough draft of the realistic content is always better than Greek text. If you have a copywriting team, work closely with them throughout this process and have them develop content as you go so the front-end development team can flow the copy into the prototype as it's built.

Continually ask yourself: what content needs to be shown here, what interactions need to take place, and where do we want the user to go next?

## Questions to Ask While Evaluating and Critiquing Wireframes

Now that we have a working prototype, we can use the following questions to help identify any potential user experience issues that will need to be solved. Create a list of these issues so that they can be addressed later.

- *Is it easy for potential users to find their path and accomplish their end goals?* Would a user be able to navigate from point A to point B without difficulty?
- *Are objects behaving as you would expect them to?* As you interact with objects, are things behaving consistently from page to page throughout the experience?
- *Is there anything that should be added or removed?* Are there key pieces of content or calls-to-action that are missing from a page?
- *Are things labeled clearly? Do interactive elements clearly convey their intention?* Does everything make sense? Are buttons and links clearly worded and actionable? Do things imply their function clearly (e.g., do buttons look clickable)?
- *Are there any important interactions or state changes that are currently missing?* Are all the different states of the interface accounted for? What happens if a user generates an error? What happens if data is missing for a specific piece of functionality?
- *Are the interactions and animations elegant and seamless?* Does interactivity add to the experience instead of degrade it? Are there microinteractions such as system alerts, error notices, or other small interface interactions that could be made more delightful?

## Designing Out the Details

Now it's time to design the detailed screens and interactions for the remainder of the experience.

### Don't Just Skin the Wires

There's a tendency at this point for the designers working on the project to take the wireframes literally, but you'll want to ensure that this final design phase doesn't become an exercise of coloring in the boxes.

Design at this stage is about polishing details and interactions so that the end result is user delight. In Chapter 4, we talked about how important things like error text, interface animations, and other subtle microinteractions were to the overall experience. It's during this detailed design phase that you have an opportunity to make them better.

Prioritize the list of issues/concerns that you documented during your detailed review of the wireframes and work with your team to iterate potential design solutions to the problems.

If there are missing components that need to be designed, make sure they're accounted for and that all creative assets are organized and accessible.

During this phase, I find it valuable to print out each individual interface screen designs as they're completed and hang them side-by-side on a wall. This allows you to take a systems view of the entire digital experience. Look for consistency of design patterns and visual elements, and try to identify areas of the experience that feel under-designed or formulaic.

Write questions or feedback on each individual screen as you review them. That way the designer has notes that they can later use to address your feedback.

As detailed designs are complete, work with the development team to implement them into the existing code base. At this point your prototype is getting close to a final product.

## Reviewing the Final Product and Making It Better

When the development team is done with implementation and build, the product is ready to move into the QA and testing phase. At this point, it's really tempting to rest on your laurels, but avoid that temptation.

### The Last Mile Should Be the Hardest

Any runner will tell you that if you're really giving your all, the last mile should be the most difficult one. Continue to attack your work and strive to make it better.

Don't make this phase just about testing functionality; make it about improving the entire user experience. Removing those final stumbling blocks to make things more elegant and simplified.

The truth is there are a lot of things you won't notice until you actually see the final product, and that's ok.

If you're not saying, *how could we make this better?* two weeks prior to launch, then you're not trying hard enough.

This is your last chance to really improve things before we move onto user testing. Make the most of it.

### Testing Your Assumptions

Now that you've got a working product, it's time to put it in front of real users and get feedback on it. This is where the rubber meets the road.

You might be thinking that user testing isn't the responsibility of the creative director, and if you're at a company that has a usability team that handles the user testing process, then great—let them have a go at it.

But if your company doesn't have a usability testing practice, then get ready to get your hands dirty. If you're responsible for user delight, then you need to have experience watching users interact with the work you created.

## A Simple and Lean Approach to User Testing

For our purposes, we only need 5–10 people to test with. We're not trying to do a giant empirical study, we just want to get our prototypes in front of real users and observe them as they use it.

When recruiting test participants, you can follow the same process you did with user research. In fact, you can even call back the same folks you interviewed during the research phase and see if they want to participate in user testing.

You can also recruit by posting your screener to craigslist, or ask the client to provide a few people who would be interested in coming in for testing.

To run a user test, you don't need a big lab. Simply reserve a conference room for a day and schedule your users with 30 minutes between each.

Prior to the testing day create a simple testing script. That script should set the scenario and outline the tasks you'd like the user to complete. These scenarios should be based upon the key actions the user needs to take on the website to complete their goals.

A scenario script might look something like this.

---

Thank you for participating in this study. The goal of this study is to observe users as they interact with a prototype of BigCo Insurance's new website. In just a moment, I'll be giving you a scenario and a few corresponding tasks and then observing as you try to complete them. Feel free to talk through your actions as you take them, but I won't be able to offer any help or assistance during the process.

*Scenario 1*: As a homeowner, you noticed that your roof appeared to be missing shingles after a recent large storm. BigCo Insurance holds your homeowner's policy.

*Task 1*: Using this website, try to find out if storm damage is covered by your homeowner's policy.

*Task 2*: Now that you know storm damage is covered, I'd like you to attempt to file a claim with the insurance company and get a repair scheduled.

---

Once you've given them the tasks, simply observe their actions. So that you're not taking notes the entire time, I'd recommend using a screen-recording application like Silverback or Camtasia.

FIGURE 8.2    **A mobile testing rig makes user testing video capture easy.**

For recording user activity on a mobile device, you can buy an inexpensive mobile rig like Mr. Tappy or a MOD1000 (see Figure 8.2) that allows you to easily mount the camera above the phone.

As they're trying to complete the tasks you assigned them, watch for areas of difficulty, and see if there are potential hurdles that make it hard for them to complete their task. Make note of the tasks they couldn't complete, or parts of the design that posed trouble.

Repeat the process with each test participant. Once you're done with testing, you should have a clear view of potential usability issues, and can start working toward design solutions that solve the problem.

## Designing in Agile Environment

There are two major methodologies in use when it comes to managing the process of designing and building digital experiences: 1) waterfall method and 2) agile method.

The waterfall method is a sequential design process that strives to document requirements at the maximum level of clarity at each individual phase of the process and get approval on those requirements at the end of each phase before moving on to the next. This was the dominant methodology for digital product design for a number of years.

In the real world, it often looked something like this: Business analysts would create detailed specifications and requirements documents (sometimes hundreds of pages long), then developers would build based on those requirements. And then after everything was built, designers would come in and clean things up a little bit.

Then it would be released to users who found that not only did it not solve their problems, but also that it was difficult to use.

This approach was a recipe for disaster. Luckily, in today's world, few firms take this approach and it's much more likely that design acts as a bridge between requirements, user needs, and development/engineering instead of only appearing at the end.

That being said, many firms still use the traditional waterfall method of defining requirements, then completing all design work, and then only starting development once all design is complete. I don't recommend taking this approach.

As a reaction against the potential pitfalls of the waterfall methodology, Agile was created to be more developer-centric, iterative, and incremental. In an agile process, projects are broken into smaller sprints (5 or 10 days) and progress is measured in completed code. Business requirements are kept lightweight and developers play a key role in the process of defining a solution.

Over the last five years, agile has become the de facto standard development process for many organizations both large and small.

While agencies have been slow to adopt this approach, it's much more common now than it was before and as a creative director it's important to understand what an agile approach to design looks like.

## Designing in an Agile Environment

So how does the design process change in the world of agile? First, the project will be broken down into a series of sprints. These sprints will likely last five days. A standard design sprint will look something like this.

- *Day 1: Research and problem definition*—On the first day, it's all about research. Review what you know about the users, talk to any stakeholders that may have valuable insight, and understand any constraints that you may have to operate under.
- *Day 2: Sketches and iterations*—The second day is all about low fidelity iteration. Sketch, sketch, sketch, and then sketch some more. Then meet with the core team and discuss potential solutions.
- *Day 3: Initial design concepting*—The third day is all about taking the low fidelity sketch that you decided held the most promise and bringing it to life.
- *Day 4: Polish and refine*—The fourth day is your opportunity to polish and refine the design concept. Work over the rough edges. Think through the interactions and make it better. In really nimble organizations, a development team may even build a functioning prototype on Day 4.

- *Day 5: Show and gather feedback*—The last day is about gathering feedback. If you have a functioning prototype, then get it in front of representative users and give them a scenario to complete. If you're only working with static design, then it will require a bit more imagination for the user to pretend to interact with the design, but you can still gather feedback.

This design sprint approach is ideal for highly complex user interface projects like web-based and mobile apps that have a really heavy development component. The big advantage is that you're getting real feedback on a weekly basis instead of waiting until the very end of a design process.

## Reference

Brand, S. 1994. *How Buildings Learn*. Viking Penguin, New York.

# Chapter 9

# Presenting Your Work Like a Pro

*A presentation has to share just enough of the process so that someone who has not been a participant can understand the 'inevitability' of the solution, and that the solution is the culmination of a rigorous and systematic investigation of all reasonable possibilities.*

**Saul Bass**
(quoted in Jennifer Bass and Pat Kirkham,
Saul Bass: A Life in Film & Design, *2011*)

In the introduction to this book, I mentioned that the job of a digital creative director is at its heart a rhetorical one. The only way to succeed in this role is to convince skeptical clients and stakeholders that the path you're recommending will lead them to success.

Often this part of the job is the most difficult for those that come from a design background. What led you to success early in your career was your ability as a craftsman and now all of a sudden you're asked to sell a design concept to a crowd of skeptics.

Some people reading this will be afraid of public speaking. Just the idea will bring butterflies to their stomach. I felt the same way when I first started. But the ability to present is one of the most important skills a creative director has.

The key to overcoming your fears and presenting your work like a pro is simple. It's called preparation.

The first thing you need to realize is that the people want you to succeed and it's ok to be nervous. The truth is if you're nervous, the work is good, and you appear likable, then the client is going to be rooting for you to do a great job.

You're there to help them evaluate the work in a strategic way and guide them on the type of feedback that they need to provide. You also want to present the hard work of your team in a way that represents it in the best light possible and positions you as an expert who they can trust.

## Understand the Environment and the Audience

One of the most common pieces of advice you'll see is to stand up when presenting. And this is good advice.

However, there are few times when it doesn't make sense. The act of standing up to present adds a level of formality that may make the client feel awkward if the meeting is informal in nature. If it's just you and the client in a small room, it may be wise to scrap the projector and review the presentation on your laptop or iPad instead.

However, if you're in the client's conference room and their entire executive team is there, then they want a dog and pony show. They expect a level of formality, and will be disappointed if you don't provide it.

## Don't Just Show the Work. Tell a Story

The first time I presented something to a client, I botched it. I simply plugged in the projector, put the work on screen, and asked what they thought.

For the next 45 minutes they managed to rip on everything from the color choices I made, to the navigation placement, to the photography I selected. I walked out of the room fuming at how illogical they were and how bad their feedback was.

It wasn't their fault that the meeting went off the rails. It was mine. I didn't introduce the work in a way that explained my rationale, or speak to their goals, or even tell them what type of feedback I needed. The meeting became about their personal likes and dislikes instead of how the design met their user's needs.

Learn from my mistakes. Don't just show your work. Present your work in the right way.

## What to Include in Your Creative Presentation

A good creative presentation should create a narrative around the work you are presenting. We'll start with the high-level context and goals, and then move into the more detailed aspects of your solution and recommendations.

By taking this approach, we can establish the parameters of the discussion and make sure the input we're getting provides value.

## Start by Setting the Context

The goal of the first part of the presentation is to set and align expectations. Let them know how many concepts you're presenting and what form those concepts will take. Let them know that not everything they're seeing will be perfect. That design is an iterative process and you want their feedback. If you're using example imagery or iconography, mention that the imagery and icons included are for placement only, but provide a good example of the tone and feeling you'd like to achieve.

You'll also want to speak to the type of the feedback you want to receive from the client. Specific examples work best.

List the questions you want them to answer. Say something like: *As you review these concepts, we'd like for you to consider the following questions: Which concept best aligns with the brand? Does this accomplish the business goals and meet the user's needs? Is the messaging on target? If you have specific concerns, please bring them up so we can address them.*

## Introduce Your Goals and How You Got to This Point

After you've set the context, we need to remind everyone of our goals. The goal should speak to why they're undertaking the project and what they're trying to accomplish. This helps set the stage for later when you talk through the rationale behind your design decisions.

Oftentimes the people that are involved in design presentations haven't been a part of the entire project from start to finish. If that's the case, be sure to include a slide explaining the process of how you got here. Let them know you did your homework—from stakeholder interviews to qualitative customer research, and detailed experience mapping. This helps to give you credibility and shows that your decisions aren't based on personal taste, but instead on research and insights.

## Reveal the Solution from the Audience's Perspective

Now it's time for the unveiling. I like to give each concept a unique name so that they're easier to remember and refer to later. The names can be simple. Pick something that can be related to the core idea of the concept like clarity, engagement, or transformation.

Start with the high-level inspiration behind the concept and then reveal the concept. Once the design is on the screen, don't give them a tour of the design elements. They can clearly see that the navigation is located at the top of the page.

Instead walk them through the experience from the user's point of view. Narrate how a user would interact and flow through the experience.

## Explain Your Rationale

As you're walking them through the experience, explain your rationale for design decisions. Talk to them about the insights that led to certain decisions, or the false starts you abandoned once you found a better design solution. Throughout this process, tie each point back to the business objectives and the goals of the project.

## Preempt Their Possible Objections

As you're preparing for your presentation, think through the specific objections they're likely to have.

If you've changed something from their brand guidelines, don't wait for them to bring it up. Address it directly and speak with confidence around the rationale for your decision. If you're taking their messaging in a new direction, explain why.

Preempt their objections and let them know it was a conscious and well-reasoned decision.

## Remember to Highlight Easily Overlooked Details

Generally design will be presented in a static form. On account of this, it's easy to overlook details and interactions that are dynamic, especially things like navigation that transforms as the user scrolls down the page, or animations that take place when the user interacts with objects. Include storyboards or animatics to help make it easier to understand.

## Don't Argue. Clarify

During every presentation, there will always be at least a few concerns raised by the client. Don't argue with them. Arguing doesn't work. It's an act of escalation when the opposite is needed.

Instead of arguing, clarify. Empathize with the other person's point of view. Understand their motivations, concerns, and feelings. Then help them understand yours. Present the facts, the assumptions, and the logic behind your stance. Nine times out of 10, your disagreement was nothing more than a miscommunication.

Try to get them away from providing prescriptive design feedback (make the logo bigger) and instead try to get them to elucidate the reasons that the logo's current size concerns them. Once you understand the concern, you can speak about your rationale for the design decision.

Make it clear you understand their concern and that you will work to address it in future iterations.

## Show How Things Will Change for the Better If They Take Your Recommendation

As you near the end of presenting, try to paint a vision toward the future. Speak about how these approaches will help their brand accomplish their goals. You want to leave them with a feeling of optimism and opportunity.

## Close by Recapping the Feedback They Provided in the Meeting and Speak About Next Steps

Once the dust has settled and you're done with your presentation, close the meeting by recapping their feedback.

Specifically mention any decisions that were made (*Sounds like we're all in agreement to move forward the first concept*) or any concerns that will be addressed in future design iterations (*We'll explore ways to add an additional area for promotion of widget X on the homepage*).

You'll also want to let them know what comes next: *From here we'll take this concept and build out a full prototype of the user experience.*

Taking this approach does two things. It lets the client know you're listening and it helps eliminate any confusion around next steps.

## How to Properly Prepare for a Creative Presentation

The first thing is to make sure you understand the goals, the business, the target audience, and the competitive space backward and forward.

Assuming you've got the background knowledge covered, create a first draft of the presentation outline. It should look something like this:

- *Introduction*
  - Explain what you'll be reviewing and set the context for what's to come
- *Our goal*
  - Remind everyone of the goals of the project
- *How we got here*
  - Review the steps you've taken in the process and provide proof that the work they'll be reviewing is the product of rigorous design and competitive research. Mention any key findings
- *Key challenges*
  - Speak about the challenges you faced in the design process
- *Concept one*
  - Review concept and show how it accomplished the goals
  - Give design rationale
  - Preempt potential objections
  - Highlight overlooked details
- *Concept two*
  - Review concept and show how it accomplished the goals
  - Give design rationale
  - Preempt potential objections
  - Highlight overlooked details
- *Next steps*
  - Let the client know the type of feedback you need and what's next in the process

Complete the outline and fill it out. After that, pull together the presentation. Just because you have a detailed outline doesn't mean you have to include paragraphs of copy in the presentation. Keep it simple and highly visual. Your goal is to tell a story, not read a bunch of bullet points off a screen.

If you're nervous, rehearse your presentation 10 times without your speaker's notes visible. If you rehearse with your speaker's notes then you'll use them as a crutch. And remember, the people in the room want you to succeed. They're rooting for you.

Presenting your work like a pro isn't rocket science, but it does require preparation, and that preparation is the difference between success and failure.

## Reference

Bass, J. and Kirkham, P. 2011. *Saul Bass: A Life in Film & Design*. Laurence King Publishing Ltd., UK.

# Chapter **10**

# Keeping Yourself Motivated and Your Team Happy

*No man needs sympathy because he has to work, because he has a burden to carry. Far and away the best prize that life offers is the chance to work hard at work worth doing.*

*Theodore Roosevelt*

Many people believe that happiness is a byproduct of what happens to us. That if I made more money, had more time, or was famous things would be better.

I don't prescribe to this belief. There have been large chunks of my life where I have been profoundly unhappy, and it resulted not from what was going on around me, but instead it was the result of my own internal response to the crashing waves and turmoil of life on planet Earth.

Unhappiness in a professional setting often derives from a lack of perspective that makes it seem like bad feedback from a client, an unprofitable project, or an employee choosing to work elsewhere is a reason to lose sleep at night.

It's the illusion that worrying about things is a valid response to a problem instead of just a way to make you feel helpless about the things in which you have little control.

I do believe that one can find happiness at work, but it's not the happiness of leisure. It's the happiness that comes from working toward the mastery of your craft.

In this chapter, we're going to talk about how to stay motivated, fight busyness, seek happiness for yourself and your team, and how to build a strong creative culture.

## Staying Motivated When It Feels Like the World Is on Your Shoulders

As you grow in your career, at some point you'll reach a level at which you dread opening your inbox. Somehow you went from 10 e-mails a day to a 100. At this point, it's easy to get discouraged. You'll want to close the browser and you'll feel disheartened at the number of things awaiting your response.

The same thing will happen to your to-do list. Where once you had only a few items on the list, now it's grown in scale and complexity. Just looking at it will give you heartburn.

### Get Used to Being Overwhelmed

This won't change. The only response is triage. You can't possibly respond to everything at the same time. So prioritize what is most important.

Pick a few really important things that you're going to do each day. These are the big items that are going to make an impact. Then make sure they happen. Come hell or high water, these things need to get done. Block off your calendar, skip meetings, put in earplugs, do whatever you need to do to get these big items complete.

If you focus on getting these big items done, then magically all the little stuff will fit in the cracks and crevices pretty painlessly. However, if you focus on filling your day with the little stuff, you'd never find room for the big stuff.

Charles Caleb Colton (1820) put it best in his little book of aphorisms called *Lacon (Or Many Things in Few Words: Addressed to Those Who Think)*.

He said: "Much may be done in those little shreds and patches of time which every day produces, and which most men throw away."

During these small windows of time that you're not working on the big things, be ruthlessly efficient and focused. Respond to 10 e-mails in 10 minutes. Knock out a few sketches for a project, or throw together a rough draft of a presentation outline. The goal isn't perfection. It's progress.

### The Value of Intensity

There's an old saying in boxing: "A round is not a round, and not all miles are created equal."

Two people can do the exact same workout, but the amount of blood, sweat, and tears they put into it can be entirely different. There's a huge difference between merely going through the motions of your workout, versus attacking your workout as if your life depended on it. It's simply a matter of intensity.

The same is true of your day-to-day work. The amount of effort you put into it is directly proportional to the end result.

You can't expect to become an exceptional creative director without exerting exceptional effort. Sadly, there are no shortcuts. The road to success is paved with intense, focused hard work over an extended period of time. Exceptional people make exceptional effort. It's rarely about talent; it's almost always about intensity.

When you take this approach, a funny thing happens. You feel pride in your work. It's no longer just a job—it's an opportunity to push yourself and achieve things you've never done before. The amount of work and passion you put into a task is directly related to the pride you feel when the job is complete.

## During Harvest Season You Work the Fields

A generation ago, my family lived off the land. They were farmers. Farming can be a hard life, and my grandfather is the definition of tough. Not in a Clint Eastwood way. There were no mean looks or quick quips. Instead my grandfather had what I refer to as *grit*.

He had the backbone and quiet fortitude to stick it out in tough times. He'd wake up at 4:00 am, even when he didn't feel like it.

Steven Pressfield (2012), in the book *The War of Art*, referred to this as being a professional. He said the difference between an amateur and a professional is that the professional does his job even when he doesn't feel like it. Artists, like farmers, know the key to success is pushing through the difficult times even when it's the last thing in the world you want to do.

When it feels like the world is on your shoulders and you're at the breaking point, just remember to keep it in perspective. Don't let being *busy* stress you out. Stay calm, keep your head down, and work through it. During harvest season, you work the fields until you're done.

## You Are a Voracious, Self-Directed Learner. Act Accordingly

At some point, you'll have done this job long enough that you'll slip into a routine. You'll stop learning and start lecturing.

This is a dangerous habit and will lead to an internal dissatisfaction that will be hard to put your finger on.

We're innate learners so it's against our nature to stop. Don't believe me? You were born with the gift of learning. By the time you were five, you'd learned the entire English language. By the age of 10, you knew algebra. Learning is something we were born to do. Never stop.

## Awards Are Great, but They Shouldn't Be What Motivates You

Creative directors love awards. In fact, I don't think I've ever gotten a resume that didn't list out the ones they won. And it's not unusual for a creative director to aim for a major award as a career goal. They think if they can just win that Cannes Gold Lion award, they'd be happy.

But what most people don't realize is that the type of goals you set for yourself can have an impact on your long-term performance and satisfaction.

By setting your goals around external validation like winning awards, you can undermine your long-term performance and satisfaction.

That's because there are two possible outcomes to this type of goal setting. If you don't win, you become discouraged and demotivated because your self-worth is based on some award given by people you've never even met. If you do win, you become less motivated to continue the hard work of self-improvement (after all you hit you won your award).

So what's the alternative? Don't strive to win awards. Instead try to become the best you can be at your craft, and the awards will follow.

Since true mastery is always beyond reach, there is always something to strive for. Even if it's as simple as being better at your job tomorrow than you were today.

Mastery is like a line that's asymptotic. The curve of the line gets closer and closer, but you never quite reach it. It's a process of continual improvement.

People who reach the pinnacle of this profession rarely care about the awards they've won. They're more interested in competing with themselves than gaining external validation.

## When the Day Is Done, Close Up Shop

I've talked a lot about the *work* aspect of what we do, but you'll never stay happy and motivated if the only walls you see are the ones in your office.

In fact, your work will suffer greatly if you never have downtime and let the muse of inspiration work her magic.

I've met people who take pride in the number of hours they work, but it's a foolish thing to keep track of. Instead work hard while working, but keep reasonable hours. Then shut off the lights, and close up the factory. There will always be more work than time if you allow it. It'll be there tomorrow when you come back.

It's only by participating fully in the experience of living a full life that we can create work that resonates. Travel, family, friends, food, great books, and new experiences are the well from which we pull forth our ideas. If the well is empty, the work will be hollow.

## A Full Night's Sleep Is the Best Preparation for a Day of Hard Work

Our industry loves to burn the midnight oil to stay up late and push through the exhaustion to eke out a bit more progress. In the short run, this may work, but you'll pay a toll in the days that follow.

A much more sustainable approach is to work until you feel like you're done. Once you're tired and the work is no longer fun, close the laptop and start again tomorrow. Go home, relax, and get a good night's sleep.

The positive benefits of getting enough sleep are well documented. A University of Michigan study showed that getting an extra hour's sleep would do more for the average person's daily happiness than getting a $60,000 raise (Barnett 2007).

It seems too easy, but a good night's rest is the simplest step you can take to being happier.

## Keeping Your Team Happy

We've talked a lot about caring for yourself, but your biggest responsibility is to your team. It's your job to create an environment where they can flourish and do work that they are proud of. A place where people have confidence that if they do good work, then good things will happen for them and for the organization.

You have to be intentional about this. If you want to keep your people happy, then you have to build a strong creative culture.

### You're Here for Them. Not the Other Way Around

One of the biggest mistakes that those new to leadership make is looking at things from their own perspective instead of that of their employees. You have to lead with the understanding that you're here to serve your team. They're not here to serve you.

Employees need three things to feel fulfilled at work. They need autonomy, mastery, and a sense of purpose. Daniel Pink (2009) covers this topic in depth in his book, *Drive: The Surprising Truth About What Motivates Us*. It's worth a read for anyone in management, but his basic argument is that the carrot-and-stick form of management that was invented by Frederick Taylor in the industrial age doesn't work for the modern knowledge worker and can actually be harmful. This idea that without the prod of reward or punishment, we'd never get off the couch and work just doesn't jive with the reality of the self-motivated people who work in the creative field. You can apply these lessons to your own team in a few ways.

Autonomy is when you allow people to self-direct their efforts and give them a level of control around their work. This means giving them clear direction, but also the freedom to figure out a solution on their own. Provide guidance and feedback, but the best creative leaders help point their team toward a solution instead of dictating it.

We talked about mastery in regard to your own motivation earlier in the chapter, but you also want your team to seek continual improvement. Think of each employee as being on a journey toward mastery, and you're his or her guide. It's your job to encourage when they're down and show them just how far they've come. It's easy in the day-to-day hustle for a young designer to feel hopeless. The journey is a long one, but you can help them. Remind them how much they have improved. Treat the work they create as a form of practice, and coach them to make it better.

One of the hardest parts of this job is to consistently keep your employees challenged at a level that fits their skillset, so they can consistently improve. This level will be different for each employee. The ideal is something that's just a notch or two higher than their average abilities. It's work that is difficult, but not impossible. This way they stay engaged and excited about the work they create.

Creating a sense of purpose is the key for building motivation. Unfortunately, the idea of purpose in companies has often been reduced into the droll mission statement that rarely inspires or motivates. But purpose operates on multiple levels. There is the organizational purpose—the reason the organization exists, but also the purpose behind individual tasks.

When the military was looking at success rates for various difficult missions over the years, they found that something called *task cohesion* was one of the most important elements in predicting successful mission outcomes.

Not surprisingly, one of the most important elements of creating task cohesion is having your team understand the reason behind the mission, and how it fits into the larger goals of the organization.

As you're assigning creative work, be sure to let the team know the why behind the task and how it fits into the organization's mission. This is especially important with thankless tasks. The short notice, fast turnaround banner ad project may not be very much fun, but if the team understands that it's a favor for one of the agency's longest tenured and high-profile clients, then they'll be much more likely to give the project the effort it deserves.

## On the Topic of Compensation

In a well-run organization, compensation is something that should largely fade into the background. The goal of any leader should be to pay people at market rate that is similar to what they would receive at another organization of similar type to do work they really enjoy.

As employees improve, you should be proactive in increasing their compensation. It's always better to offer an employee a raise before they ask for it. By the time they come to you seeking an increase in compensation, they're likely to feel undervalued.

To figure out what the market rate is, you can use online tools such as the *free salary report* at http://www.payscale.com. Simply choose the job title that best fits their role, their geographic location, and their experience. The results will be a report that shows what the average salary looks like for that person.

## How to Handle Performance Reviews

Every company has their own methodology for performance reviews, and you'll have to adapt to whatever method is used within your organization. However, that doesn't mean you can't make them more effective by ensuring that the employee is setting his or her own goals and that you're providing constant, critical feedback on a regular basis.

As part of this process, you should get used to holding a 15-minute one-on-one meeting with each direct report on a weekly basis.

## The Importance of One-on-one Meetings with Your Team Members

The goal of the one-on-one meeting is to create a free space to discuss any pressing issues, frustrations, or ideas big and small that your employees might have. It's an opportunity for you to see how they're faring and an opportunity for them to share their wins, their concerns, and their failures in a safe, friendly, and conversational environment.

If there aren't any pressing issues, then ask questions like the below to start the conversation:

- Do you feel your making progress toward the goals you set for yourself for this year? How can I provide support?
- Are you enjoying the projects you're working on? Are they challenging enough?
- If you were me, what changes would you make to the way we do things?
- What's not fun about working here?

These meetings should be the employee's opportunity to get their problems and solutions in front of someone who can deal with them.

It's easy to cancel these meetings when you're busy, but you shouldn't give in to that temptation. Keep them on the calendar. They're the best way to foster open communication between you and the individuals on your team.

## Take Blame. Give Credit

The business world has a hero complex. Founders and leaders get way more credit than they deserve. But the reality is that success only happens when a strong team works together to do amazing things.

It's easy as a creative leader to believe in your own heroics and pat yourself on the back for what you've accomplished. This should be avoided. Try instead to take the blame when things go wrong, and give credit when things go right.

Simple things such as sending an e-mail out to the company after a successful project wins an award that praises each individual involved in the project, the role they played, and how it led to success can mean a lot to the people on the receiving end.

## Don't Try to *Spin* Bad News

There will be times when things go badly. You'll work hard on a pitch and lose the business. The team will have presented work that the client loved at the in-person meeting, only to hear back a week later that they now hate it. Other times, it might be that you lost a key team member to a competitive agency.

There are two paths you can take when things like this happen. The first path is to try to put a positive spin on it. Act like a cheerleader, tell people to look on the bright side, and try to give a motivational speech, even when it's clear that something bad happened. This works in the movies, but in the real world most people will see through the spin and it will come across as insincere.

The better path is to be completely honest. Let them know what happened. Don't pull any punches. Give them the same level of transparency that you'd want if you were in their shoes. Tell them you know what happened sucks, but that you'll get through it.

Winston Churchill once said, "If you're going through hell. Keep going" (*Forbes* 2012). That's the message you'll want to give to your team when you inevitably hit a really rough patch.

Be honest, but let them know that this too shall pass and the future will be better than the present. Don't try to persuade them with *spin*. They won't buy it.

## Proactively Seek Out Talent. Don't Wait for Resumes to Come to You

Inevitably the day will come when a team member leaves. Hopefully it's to take a new opportunity that will help them take the next step in their career.

When this happens, you'll have to recruit someone to replace them. Notice I didn't say hire someone. The fact is: talented people have options. If you want them to work for you, you'll need to find them and recruit them.

Hiring a new employee is a big investment, and potentially a risky one as well. This is made more difficult because the digital industry is growing, and is highly competitive. There are a lot of good companies vying for a limited number of exceptional people.

The single biggest differentiator a creative team can have versus its competition is the talent level of their people.

So how do you go about getting more talented people than your competition?

Don't just rely on a job posting. Scout, identify, and recruit talent proactively. It's easier than ever to look for talent. You can identify potential employees with nothing more than a few minutes searching LinkedIn, Dribble, and other online portfolio tools.

Also, ask your employees and friends to help you find talent. See if there is anyone they know from previous experiences who would strengthen the team.

You'll also want to build good relationships with the creative/design schools around you. They have dedicated staff focused on placement. Use their resources to help you identify entry-level talent.

Changing from a hiring mindset to a recruiting mindset should also shift the way you approach the interview process. Each touch point with a potential hire is an interaction with your brand.

If the applicant has to answer a series of generic preinterview questions by e-mail, is blown off by a distracted team member when they come for the in-person interview, and has to sit uncomfortably in the lobby for an extended period of time; then the chances are the applicant is going to judge your company based on those interactions.

And if those interactions are negative, then you're at a disadvantage from the start. Talented people aren't really *hired* by companies, they *choose* to work there. If you give them a reason to say no, chances are they'll take it.

## Each New Hire either Strengthens or Weakens Culture

During this process, remember that each person you add to the team either strengthens or weakens the company culture. There's no middle ground when it comes to new employees.

As part of the interview process, make sure they meet with at least two to three key team members. The other team members don't need to assess their acumen for the position. Instead ask them to seek out culture fit. Would this person excel in this environment? Do their values and approach to work align with the organizations?

A strong culture fit doesn't mean that the person you're hiring is like the other people who work there, or that they would spend their weekends hanging out together. Focus on their core values, personality traits, and approach to work.

Is your workplace hyperaggressive and assertive? If so, a passive introvert likely won't feel very comfortable. If your corporate culture is full of self-starters who deplore bureaucracy, then someone who previously worked in a big, bureaucratic company might not be the best fit.

Hiring is the most important activity you'll undertake. Spend the time to find the right person and you'll save yourself a lot of time and prevent a lot of future trouble.

## Be the Type of Boss You'd Want to Work For

My last piece of advice is simple. It's a version of the golden rule—be the type of leader and the type of person that you'd want to work for. Work hard to understand what it feels like to work for you and try to build an environment that engenders trust, loyalty, and pride with those that you share the trenches with.

The best compliment you can receive as a leader is someone wanting to work for you again. Not because they have to, but because they want to.

Good luck on your journey.

## References

Barnett, R. February 15, 2007. How to be a happier mom: 8 ways to focus on the positive. *CNN*. http://www.cnn.com/2007/HEALTH/parenting/02/15/par.happier.mom/index.html. Accessed on January 28, 2016.

Colton, C. C. 1820. *Lacon, Or, Many Things in Few Words: Addressed to Those Who Think*. Longman, Hurst, Rees, Orme, and Brown, London.

Forbes Magazine. 09 May 2012, *Forbes*. http://www.forbes.com/sites/geoffloftus/2012/05/09/if-youre-going-through-hell-keep-going-winston-churchill/#2965c9903a3b. Accessed on April 18, 2016.

Pink, D. H. 2009. *Drive: The Surprising Truth About What Motivates Us*. Riverhead, New York, NY.

Pressfield, S. 2012. *The War of Art: Break through the Blocks and Win Your Inner Creative Battles*. Black Irish Entertainment, New York.

# Index

9781138847514